THE LARAMIE PROJECT

BY MOISÉS KAUFMAN
AND THE MEMBERS OF TECTONIC
THEATER PROJECT

★

★

DRAMATISTS
PLAY SERVICE
INC.

THE LARAMIE PROJECT
Copyright © 2001, Moisés Kaufman

All Rights Reserved

SPECIAL NOTE

The following acknowledgment must appear on the title page in all programs distributed in connection with performances of the Play:

The US West World Premiere was produced by
The Denver Center Theatre Company
Donovan Marley, Artistic Director
in association with
Tectonic Theater Project
Moisés Kaufman, Artistic Director.

Originally produced in New York City at the Union Square Theatre
by Roy Gabay and Tectonic Theater Project
in association with Gayle Francis and the Araca Group
Associate Producers: Mara Isaacs and Hart Sharp Entertainment.

The Laramie Project was developed in part with the support of
The Sundance Theatre Laboratory.

The following acknowledgment must appear in all programs distributed in connection with performances of the Play:

THE LARAMIE PROJECT
Written by Moisés Kaufman
and the Members of Tectonic Theater Project

HEAD WRITER
Leigh Fondakowski

ASSOCIATE WRITERS
Stephen Belber, Greg Pierotti, Stephen Wangh

DRAMATURGS
Amanda Gronich, Sarah Lambert, John McAdams,
Maude Mitchell, Andy Paris, Barbara Pitts, Kelli Simpkins

In addition, the "Author's Note" included in this book and biographies for Moisés Kaufman, Leigh Fondakowski, Stephen Belber, Greg Pierotti and Stephen Wangh must appear in all programs distributed in connection with performances of the Play.

THE LARAMIE PROJECT

WRITTEN BY MOISÉS KAUFMAN
AND THE MEMBERS OF TECTONIC THEATER PROJECT

HEAD WRITER
Leigh Fondakowski

ASSOCIATE WRITERS
Stephen Belber, Greg Pierotti, Stephen Wangh

DRAMATURGS
Amanda Gronich, Sarah Lambert, John McAdams,
Maude Mitchell, Andy Paris, Barbara Pitts, Kelli Simpkins

*Dedicated to the people of Laramie, Wyoming
and to Matthew Shepard*

ACKNOWLEDGMENTS

The members of Tectonic Theater Project and Moisés Kaufman thank the following people for their contributions to *The Laramie Project*:

Michael Emerson, Sarah Lambert, Maude Mitchell, Molly Powell, James Asher, Dave McKennan, Ledlie Hoffstedler and Jan Leslie Harding for their participation at different stages of the play's development.

In Laramie, the staff of the Albany County Courthouse, the faculty and staff of the University of Wyoming Theater Department, Catherine Connolly and her family, Rob DeBree, Philip Dubois, Tiffany Edwards, Reggie and Mike Fluty and their family, Ben Fritzen, Matt Galloway, Susanna Goodin, Larry and Carolyne Hazlett, Rebecca Hilliker and Rich Nelson, Stephen Mead Johnson, Phil Labrie, Beth Loffreda, Bob McKee, Bear and Jeri McKinney, Matt Mickelson, Jeffrey Montgomery, Garrett Neergaard, Romaine Patterson, Gene Pratt, Cathy Renna, Zackie Salmon, Jessica Sanchez, Father Roger Schmit, Jedadiah Schultz, Jonas Slonaker, Rulon Stacey, Trish and Ron Steger, Zubaida Ula, Harry Woods and all the people of Laramie, Wyoming, who so generously opened their hearts and minds to us.

Robert Redford, Philip Himberg, Ken Brecher, Robert Blacker, Beth Nathanson, Shirley Fishman, and the staff of the Sundance Theater Lab. They flew us to their beautiful oasis in the Utah mountains and gave us an artistic environment in which to work. Large sections of this play were written there.

In New York, Jim Nicola and New York Theatre Workshop for their belief in our work and their invitation to participate in their summer retreat at Dartmouth, where even more of this play was written. Dominick Balletta and Performance Associates for their guidance and work on our behalf. Lynne Soffer and Walton Wilson for their excellence.

In Denver, Donovan Marley, Barbara Sellers, Rick Barbour, Chris Wiger and everyone at the Denver Center Theatre Company for producing the World Premiere of *The Laramie Project*. They took on a play that was very much in progress — in fact, it had no third act — and gave us a home to finish it.

For their courageous support of the development of the play, we thank Joan Shigekawa and the Rockefeller Foundation, Rob Marx and the Fan Fox and Leslie R. Samuels Foundation, the New York State Council on the Arts, the Jeanne M. Sullivan and Joseph P. Sullivan Foundation, Anne Milliken and Leon Levy.

Roy Gabay, Gayle Francis, Mara Isaacs, Hank Unger, Mike Rego, Matt Rego, John Hart and Jeff Sharp, who had the vision and knowhow to bring *The Laramie Project* to the New York stage.

Joe and Jeanne Sullivan, for their generous and unwavering support of our creative process.

Peter Cane and Joyce Ketay for their continuous support and advice; Alan Schuster for his interest and his beautiful theater; and Kevin McAnarney for getting the word out.

To the following people and institutions for their wonderful attention to the very pragmatic things that made *The Laramie Project* possible: Marta Bell, Mérida Castillejo, Randall Kent Cohn, Gino Dilonio, Jonathan Ferrantelli, Michael Honda, Christy Meyer, Megan Spooner, Anne Stott, Courtney Watson, the Atlantic Theater Company, Access Theater and the Church of St. Paul and St. Andrew.

AUTHOR'S NOTE
by Moisés Kaufman

The Laramie Project was written through a unique collaboration by Tectonic Theater Project. During the year-and-a-half development of the play, members of the company and I traveled to Laramie six times to conduct interviews with the people of the town. We transcribed and edited the interviews, then conducted several workshops in which the members of the company presented material and acted as dramaturgs in the creation of the play.

As the volume of material grew with each additional trip to Laramie, a small writers' group from within the company began to work closely with me to further organize and edit the material, conduct additional research in Laramie, and collaborate on the writing of the play. This group was led by Leigh Fondakowski as Head Writer, with Stephen Belber and Greg Pierotti as Associate Writers.

As we got closer to the play's first production in Denver, the actors, including Stephen Belber and Greg Pierotti, turned their focus to performance, while Leigh Fondakowski continued to work with me on drafts of the play, as did Stephen Wangh, who by then had joined us as an Associate Writer and "bench coach."

INTRODUCTION
by Moisés Kaufman

After all, not to create only, or found only,
But to bring perhaps from afar what is already founded,
To give it our own identity, average, limitless, free.

—Walt Whitman

There are moments in history when a particular event brings the various ideologies and beliefs prevailing in a culture into sharp focus. At these junctures, the event becomes a lightning rod of sorts, attracting and distilling the essence of these philosophies and convictions. By paying careful attention in moments like this to people's words, one is able to hear the way these prevailing ideas affect not only individual lives but also the culture at large.

The trials of Oscar Wilde were such an event. When I read the transcripts of the trials (while preparing to write *Gross Indecency*), I was struck by the clarity with which they illuminated an entire culture. In these pages one can see not only a community dealing with the problem that Wilde presented, but in their own words, Victorian men and women telling us — three generations later — about the ideologies, idiosyncrasies and philosophies that formed the pillars of that culture and ruled their lives.

The brutal murder of Matthew Shepard was another event of this kind. In its immediate aftermath, the nation launched into a dialogue that brought to the surface how we think and talk about homosexuality, sexual politics, education, class, violence, privileges and rights, and the difference between tolerance and acceptance.

The idea for *The Laramie Project* originated in my desire to learn more about why Matthew Shepard was murdered; about what happened that night; about the town of Laramie. The idea of listening to the citizens talk really interested me. How is Laramie different from the rest of the country and how is it similar?

11

Shortly after the murder, I posed the question to my company, Tectonic Theater Project: What can we as theatre artists do as a response to this incident? And, more concretely: Is theatre a medium that can contribute to the national dialogue on current events?

These concerns fall squarely within Tectonic Theater Project's mission. Every project that we undertake as a company has two objectives: 1) to examine the subject matter at hand; and 2) to explore theatrical language and form. In an age when film and television are constantly redefining and refining their tools and devices, the theater has too often remained entrenched in the 19th-century traditions of realism and naturalism.

In this sense, our interest was to continue to have a dialogue on both how the theatre speaks and how it is created. Thus, I was very interested in this model: a theatre company travels somewhere, talks to people and returns with what they saw and heard to create a play.

At the time I also happened to run across a Brecht essay I had not read in a long time, "The Street Scene." In it Brecht uses as a model the following situation: "an eyewitness demonstrating to a collection of people how a traffic accident took place." He goes on to build a theory about his "epic theatre" based on this model. The essay gave me an idea about how to deal with this project, both in terms of its creation and its aesthetic vocabulary.

So in November 1998, four weeks after the murder of Matthew Shepard, nine members of Tectonic Theater Project and I traveled to Laramie, Wyoming, to collect interviews that might become material for a play. Little did we know that we would devote two years of our lives to this project. We returned to Laramie six times over the course of the next year and a half and conducted over two hundred interviews.

This play opened in Denver at the Denver Center Theater in February 2000. Then it moved to the The Union Square Theatre in New York City in May 2000. And in November 2000 we took the play to Laramie.

12

The experience of working on *The Laramie Project* has been one of great sadness, great beauty and, perhaps most importantly, great revelations — about our nation, about our ideas, about ourselves.

THE LARAMIE PROJECT received its world premiere at The Ricketson Theatre by the Denver Center Theatre Company (Donovan Marley, Artistic Director) in association with Tectonic Theater Project (Moisés Kaufman, Artistic Director; Jeffrey LaHoste, Managing Director) in Denver, Colorado, on February 19, 2000. It was directed by Moisés Kaufman; the set design was by Robert Brill; the lighting design was by Betsy Adams; the original music was by Peter Golub; the sound design was by Craig Breitenbach; the video and slides were by Martha Swetzoff; the costume design was by Moe Schell; the assistant director was Leigh Fondakowski; and the project advisor was Stephen Wangh. The cast was as follows:

Stephen Belber — Himself, Doc O'Connor, Matt Galloway, Anonymous Friend of Aaron McKinney, Bill McKinney, Andrew Gomez, Fred Phelps, Mormon Spiritual Advisor, Conrad Miller, Narrator, Ensemble.

Amanda Gronich — Herself, Eileen Engen (ACT ONE), Marge Murray, Baptist Minister, Trish Steger, Shadow, Newsperson, Narrator, Ensemble.

Mercedes Herrero — Reggie Fluty, Rebecca Hilliker, Waitress, Newsperson, Narrator, Ensemble.

John McAdams — Moisés Kaufman, Philip Dubois (ACT ONE), Stephen Mead Johnson, Murdock Cooper, Jon Peacock, Dennis Shepard, Harry Woods, Narrator, Ensemble.

Andy Paris — Himself, Jedadiah Schultz, Doug Laws, Dr. Cantway, Matt Mickelson, Russell Henderson, Aaron McKinney, Philip Dubois (ACT TWO), Kerry Drake, Narrator, Ensemble.

Greg Pierotti — Himself, Sgt. Hing, Phil LaBrie, Father Roger Schmit, Rulon Stacey, Detective Sgt. Rob DeBree, Jonas Slonaker, Narrator, Ensemble.

Barbara Pitts — Herself, Catherine Connolly, April Silva, Zubaida Ula, Sherry Aenonson, Lucy Thompson, Eileen Engen (ACT TWO), Narrator, Ensemble.

Kelli Simpkins — Leigh Fondakowski, Zackie Salmon, Alison Sears, Romaine Patterson, Aaron Kreifels, Tiffany Edwards, Narrator, Ensemble.

THE LARAMIE PROJECT subsequently opened Off-Broadway at The Union Square Theatre (Alan J. Schuster and Margaret Cotter, Managing Directors) in New York City on May 18, 2000. It was produced by Roy Gabay and Tectonic Theater Project in association with Gayle Francis and the Araca Group; Associate Producers Mara Isaacs and Hart Sharp Entertainment. It was directed by Moisés Kaufman; the set design was by Robert Brill; the lighting design was by Betsy Adams; the original music was by Peter Golub; the video and slides were by Martha Swetzoff; the costume design was by Moe Schell; the assistant director was Leigh Fondakowski; and the project advisor was Stephen Wangh. The cast was as follows:

Stephen Belber — Himself, Doc O'Connor, Matt Galloway, Anonymous Friend of Aaron McKinney, Bill McKinney, Andrew Gomez, Fred Phelps, Mormon Spiritual Advisor, Conrad Miller, Narrator, Ensemble.

Amanda Gronich — Herself, Eileen Engen (ACT ONE), Marge Murray, Baptist Minister, Trish Steger, Shadow, Newsperson, Narrator, Ensemble.

Mercedes Herrero — Reggie Fluty, Rebecca Hilliker, Waitress, Newsperson, Narrator, Ensemble.

John McAdams — Moisés Kaufman, Philip Dubois (ACT ONE), Stephen Mead Johnson, Murdock Cooper, Jon Peacock, Dennis Shepard, Harry Woods, Narrator, Ensemble.

Andy Paris — Himself, Jedadiah Schultz, Doug Laws, Dr. Cantway, Matt Mickelson, Russell Henderson, Aaron McKinney, Philip Dubois (ACT TWO), Kerry Drake, Narrator, Ensemble.

Greg Pierotti — Himself, Sgt. Hing, Phil LaBrie, Father Roger Schmit, Rulon Stacey, Detective Sgt. Rob DeBree, Jonas Slonaker, Narrator, Ensemble.

Barbara Pitts — Herself, Catherine Connolly, April Silva, Zubaida Ula, Sherry Aenonson, Lucy Thompson, Eileen Engen (ACT TWO), Narrator, Ensemble.

Kelli Simpkins — Leigh Fondakowski, Zackie Salmon, Alison Sears, Romaine Patterson, Aaron Kreifels, Tiffany Edwards, Narrator, Ensemble.

THE LARAMIE PROJECT CHARACTERS

AARON KREIFELS — University student. 19 years old.

AARON MCKINNEY — One of the perpetrators. 21 years old. A roofer.

ALISON MEARS — Volunteer for a social service agency in town. 50s. Very good friend of Marge Murray.

AMANDA GRONICH — Member of Tectonic Theater Project.

ANDREW GOMEZ — Latino from Laramie. 20s.

ANDY PARIS — Member of Tectonic Theater Project.

ANONYMOUS FRIEND OF AARON MCKINNEY'S — 20s. Works for the railroad.

APRIL SILVA — Bisexual university student. 19 years old.

BAILIFF

BAPTIST MINISTER — Originally from Texas. 50s.

BARBARA PITTS — Member of Tectonic Theater Project.

BILL MCKINNEY — Father of Aaron McKinney. 40s. Truck driver.

CAL RERUCHA — Prosecuting attorney. 50s.

CATHERINE CONNOLLY — Out lesbian professor at the university. 40s.

CONRAD MILLER — Car mechanic. 30s.

DENNIS SHEPARD — Father of Matthew Shepard. 40s. Wyoming native.

DOC O'CONNOR — Limousine driver and local entrepreneur. 50s.

DR. CANTWAY — Emergency room doctor at Ivinson Memorial Hospital in Laramie. 50s.

DOUG LAWS — Stake Ecclesiastical leader for the Mormon church in Laramie. 50s. A professor at the University of Wyoming.

EMAIL SENDER

FATHER ROGER SCHMIT — Catholic Priest. 40s. Very outspoken.

GIL AND EILEEN ENGEN — Ranchers. He is in his 60s, she is in her 50s.

GOVERNOR JIM GERINGER — Republican Governor. 45 years old.

GREG PIEROTTI — Member of Tectonic Theater Project.

HARRY WOODS — Gay Laramie resident. 52 years old.

JEDADIAH SCHULTZ — University student. 19 years old.

JEFFREY LOCKWOOD — Laramie resident. 40s.

JEN — Friend of Aaron McKinney. In her early 20s.

JON PEACOCK — Matthew Shepard's academic adviser. Late 30s. Political science professor.

JONAS SLONAKER — Gay man. 40s.

JURORS AND FOREPERSON

KERRY DRAKE — Reporter with the Caspar *Star Tribune.* 40s.

KRISTIN PRICE — Girlfriend of Aaron McKinney. 20s. Tennessee accent.

LEIGH FONDAKOWSKI — Member of Tectonic Theater Project.

LUCY THOMPSON — Grandmother of Russell Henderson. 60s. Working-class woman who provided a popular day-care service for the town.

MARGE MURRAY — Reggie's mother. 70s. She has had emphysema for many years but continues to smoke.

MATT GALLOWAY — Bartender at The Fireside Bar. 20s. Student at the University of Wyoming.

MATT MICKELSON — Owner of The Fireside. 30s.

MEDIA/NEWSPAPER PEOPLE

MERCEDES HERRERO— Member of Tectonic Theater Project.

MOISÉS KAUFMAN — Member of Tectonic Theater Project.

MORMON HOME TEACHER TO RUSSELL HENDERSON — 60s.

MURDOCK COOPER — Rancher. 50s. Resident of Centennial, a nearby town.

PHIL LABRIE — A friend of Matthew Shepard. Late 20s. Eastern European accent.

PHILIP DUBOIS — President of the University of Wyoming. 40s.

PRIEST AT THE FUNERAL

REBECCA HILLIKER — Head of the theater department at the University of Wyoming. 40s. Midwestern accent.

REGGIE FLUTY — The policewoman who responded to the 911 call and discovered Matthew at the fence. 40s.

REVEREND FRED PHELPS — Minister from Kansas. 60s.

ROB DEBREE — Detective Sgt. for the Albany County Sheriff's department. 40s. Chief investigator for the Matthew Shepard murder.

ROMAINE PATTERSON — Lesbian. 21 years old.

RULON STACEY — CEO Poudre Valley Hospital in Fort Collins, Colorado. 40s. Mormon.

RUSSELL HENDERSON — One of the perpetrators. 19 years old.

SGT. HING — Detective at the Laramie police department. 40s.

SHADOW — DJ at the Fireside. African American man. 30 years old.

SHANNON — Friend of Aaron McKinney. In his early 20s.

SHERRY AANENSON — Russell Henderson's landlord. 40s.

SHERRY JOHNSON — Administrative assistant at the University. 40s.

STEPHEN BELBER — Member of Tectonic Theater Project.

STEPHEN MEAD JOHNSON — Unitarian minister. 50s.

TIFFANY EDWARDS — Local reporter. 20s.
TRISH STEGER — Romaine's sister. 40s.
TWO JUDGES
WAITRESS — Looks like Debbie Reynolds.
ZACKIE SALMON — Administrator at the University of Wyoming.
   Lesbian. 40s. Texas accent.
ZUBAIDA ULA — Muslim woman in Laramie. 20s.

NOTE: When a character's name is not given (e.g., "Friend of Aaron McKinney," "Baptist Minister," etc.), it is at the person's request.

TIME

1998–1999.

PLACE

Laramie, Wyoming, USA.

ABOUT THE STAGING

The set is a performance space. There are a few tables and chairs. Costumes and props are always visible. The basic costumes are the ones worn by the company of actors. Costumes to portray the people of Laramie should be simple: a shirt, a pair of glasses, a hat. The desire is to suggest, not recreate. Along the same lines, this play should be an actor-driven event. Costume changes, set changes and anything else that happens on the stage should be done by the company of actors.

ABOUT THE TEXT

When writing this play, we used a technique I developed called "moment work." It is a method to create and analyze theater from a structuralist (or "tectonic") perspective. For that reason, there are no "scenes" in this play, only "moments." A "moment" does not mean a change of locale, or an entrance or exit of actors or characters. It is simply a unit of theatrical time, which is then juxtaposed with other units to convey meaning.

THE LARAMIE PROJECT

ACT ONE

MOMENT: A DEFINITION

NARRATOR. On November fourteenth, 1998, the members of Tectonic Theater Project traveled to Laramie, Wyoming and conducted interviews with the people of the town. During the next year, we would return to Laramie several times and conduct over two hundred interviews. The play you are about to see is edited from those interviews, as well as from journal entries by members of the company and other found texts. Company member Greg Pierotti.

GREG PIEROTTI. My first interview was with Detective Sergeant Hing of the Laramie Police Department. At the start of the interview he was sitting behind his desk, sitting something like this *(He transforms into Sgt. Hing.)*:

I was born and raised here.

My family is, uh, third generation.

My grandparents moved here in the early 1900s.

We've had basically three, well, my daughter makes it fourth generation.

Quite awhile … It's a good place to live. Good people — lots of space.

Now, all the towns in southern Wyoming are laid out and spaced because of the railroad came through.

It was how far they could go before having to refuel and re-water.

And, uh, Laramie was a major stopping point.

That's why the towns are spaced so far apart.

We're one of the largest states in the country, and the least populated.

REBECCA HILLIKER. There's so much space between people and towns here, so much time for reflection.

NARRATOR. Rebecca Hilliker, head of the theater department at the University of Wyoming.

REBECCA HILLIKER. You have an opportunity to be happy in your life here. I found that people here were nicer than in the Midwest, where I used to teach, because they were happy. They were glad the sun was shining. And it shines a lot here.

SGT. HING. What you have is, you have your old-time traditional-type ranchers, they've been here forever — Laramie's been the hub of where they come for their supplies and stuff like that.

EILEEN ENGEN. Stewardship is one thing all our ancestors taught us.

NARRATOR. Eileen Engen, rancher.

EILEEN ENGEN. If you don't take care of the land, then you ruin it and you lose your living. So you first of all have to take care of your land and do everything you can to improve it.

DOC O'CONNOR. I love it here.

NARRATOR. Doc O'Connor, limousine driver.

DOC O'CONNOR. You couldn't put me back in that mess out there back East. Best thing about it is the climate. The cold, the wind. They say the Wyoming wind'll drive a man insane. But you know what? It don't bother me. Well, some of the times it bothers me. But most of the time it don't.

SGT. HING. And then you got uh, the university population.

PHILIP DUBOIS. I moved here after living in a couple of big cities.

NARRATOR. Philip Dubois, president of the University of Wyoming.

PHILIP DUBOIS. I loved it there. But you'd have to be out of your mind to let your kids out after dark. And here, in the summertime, my kids play out at night till eleven o'clock and I don't think twice about it.

SGT. HING. And then you have the people who live in Laramie, basically.

ZACKIE SALMON. I moved here from rural Texas.

NARRATOR. Zackie Salmon, Laramie resident.

ZACKIE SALMON. Now, in Laramie, if you don't know a person, you will definitely know someone they know. So it can only be one degree removed at most. And for me — I love it! I mean, I love to go to the grocery store 'cause I get to visit with four or five or six people every time I go. And I don't really mind people knowing my business — 'cause what's my business? I mean, my business is basically good.

DOC O'CONNOR. I like the trains, too. They don't bother me. Well, some of the times they bother me, but most times they don't. Even though one goes by every thirteen minutes out where I live ...

NARRATOR. Doc actually lives up in Bossler. But everybody in Laramie knows him. He's also not really a doctor.

DOC O'CONNOR. They used to carry cattle ... them trains. Now all they carry is diapers and cars.

APRIL SILVA. I grew up in Cody, Wyoming.

NARRATOR. April Silva, university student.

APRIL SILVA. Laramie is better than where I grew up. I'll give it that.

SGT. HING. It's a good place to live. Good people, lots of space. Now, when the incident happened with that boy, a lot of press people came here. And one time some of them followed me out to the crime scene. And uh, well, it was a beautiful day, absolutely gorgeous day, real clear and crisp and the sky was that blue that, uh ... you know, you'll never be able to paint, it's just sky blue — it's just gorgeous. And the mountains in the background and a little snow on 'em, and this one reporter, uh, lady ... person, that, was out there, she said ...

REPORTER. "Well, who found the boy, who was out here anyway?"

SGT. HING. And I said, "Well, this is a really popular area for people to run and mountain biking's really big out here, horseback riding, it's just, well, it's close to town." And she looked at me and she said:

REPORTER. "Who in the hell would want to run out here?"

SGT. HING. And I'm thinking, "Lady, you're just missing the point." You know, all you got to do is turn around, see the mountains, smell the air, listen to the birds, just take in what's around you. And they were just — nothing but the story. I didn't feel judged, I felt that they were stupid. They're, they're missing the point — they're just missing the whole point.

23

JEDADIAH SCHULTZ. It's hard to talk about Laramie now, to tell you what Laramie is, for us.

NARRATOR. Jedadiah Schultz.

JEDADIAH SCHULTZ. If you would have asked me before, I would have told you, Laramie is a beautiful town, secluded enough that you can have your own identity ... A town with a strong sense of community — everyone knows everyone ... A town with a personality that most larger cities are stripped of. Now, after Matthew, I would say that Laramie is a town defined by an accident, a crime. We've become Waco, we've become Jasper. We're a noun, a definition, a sign. We may be able to get rid of that ... but it will sure take awhile.

MOMENT: JOURNAL ENTRIES

NARRATOR. Journal entries — members of the company. Andy Paris.

ANDY PARIS. Moisés called saying he had an idea for his next theater project. But there was a somberness to his voice, so I asked what it was all about and he told me he wanted to do a piece about what's happening in Wyoming.

NARRATOR. Stephen Belber.

STEPHEN BELBER. Leigh told me the company was thinking of going out to Laramie to conduct interviews and that they wanted me to come. But I'm hesitant. I have no real interest in prying into a town's unraveling.

NARRATOR. Amanda Gronich.

AMANDA GRONICH. I've never done anything like this in my life. How do you get people to talk to you? What do you ask?

NARRATOR. Moisés Kaufman.

MOISÉS KAUFMAN. The company has agreed that we should go to Laramie for a week and interview people.

Am a bit afraid about taking ten people in a trip of this nature. Must make some safety rules. No one works alone. Everyone carries cell phones. Have made some preliminary contacts with

Rebecca Hilliker, head of the theater department at the University of Wyoming. She is hosting a party for us our first night in Laramie and has promised to introduce us to possible interviewees.

MOMENT: REBECCA HILLIKER

REBECCA HILLIKER. I must tell you that when I first heard that you were thinking of coming here, when you first called me, I wanted to say you've just kicked me in the stomach. Why are you doing this to me?

But then I thought, that's stupid, you're not doing this to me. And more importantly, I thought about it and decided that we've had so much negative closure on this whole thing. And the students really need to talk. When this happened they started talking about it, and then the media descended and all dialogue stopped.

You know, I really love my students because they are free thinkers — and you may not like what they have to say, and you may not like their opinions, because they can be very redneck, but they are honest and they're truthful — so there's an excitement here, there's a dynamic here with my students that I never had when I was in the Midwest or in North Dakota, because there, there was so much Puritanism that dictated how people looked at the world that a lot of times they didn't have an opinion, you couldn't get them to express an opinion. And quite honestly, I'd rather have opinions that I don't like — and have that dynamic in education.

There's a student I think you should talk to. His name is Jedadiah Schultz.

MOMENT: ANGELS IN AMERICA

JEDADIAH SCHULTZ. I've lived in Wyoming my whole life. The family has been in Wyoming well ... for generations. Now when it came time to go to college, my parents can't — couldn't afford to send me to college. I wanted to study theater. And I knew that if I was going to go to college I was going to have to get on a scholarship — and so uh they have this competition each year, this Wyoming state high-school competition. And I knew that if I didn't take first place in uh duets that I wasn't gonna get a scholarship. So I went to the theater department of the university looking for good scenes and I asked one of the professors, I was like, "I need — I need a killer scene," and he was like, "Here you go, this is it." And it was from *Angels in America*.

So I read it and I knew that I could win best scene if I did a good enough job.

And when the time came I told my mom and dad so that they would come to the competition. Now you have to understand, my parents go to everything — every ballgame, every hockey game — everything I've ever done.

And they brought me into their room and told me that if I did that scene, that they would not come to see me in the competition. Because they believed that it is wrong — that homosexuality is wrong. They felt that strongly about it that they didn't want to come see their son do probably the most important thing he'd done to that point in his life. And I didn't know what to do.

I had never, ever gone against my parents' wishes. So I was kind of worried about it. But I decided to do it.

And all I can remember about the competition is that when we were done, me and my scene partner, we came up to each other and we shook hands and there was a standing ovation.

Oh, man it was amazing! And we took first place and we won. And that's how come I can afford to be here at the University, because of that scene. It was one of the best moments of my life. And my parents weren't there. And to this day, that was the one thing that my parents didn't see me do.

And thinking back on it, I think, why did I do it? Why did I oppose my parents? 'Cause I'm not gay. So why did I do it? And I guess the only honest answer I can give is that well, *(He chuckles.)* I wanted to win. It was such a good scene; it was like the best scene!

Do you know Mr. Kushner? Maybe you can tell him.

MOMENT: JOURNAL ENTRIES

NARRATOR. Company member Greg Pierotti.

GREG PIEROTTI. We arrived today in the Denver Airport and drove to Laramie — The moment we crossed the Wyoming border I swear I saw a herd of buffalo. Also, I thought it was strange that the Wyoming sign said:

THE COMPANY. WYOMING — LIKE NO PLACE ON EARTH.

GREG PIEROTTI. Instead of WYOMING — LIKE NO PLACE ELSE ON EARTH.

NARRATOR. Company member Leigh Fondakowski.

LEIGH FONDAKOWSKI. I stopped at a local inn for a bite to eat. And my waitress said to me:

WAITRESS. "Hi, my name is Debbie. I was born in 1954 and Debbie Reynolds was big then, so yes, there are a lot of us around, but I promise that I won't slap you if you leave your elbows on the table."

MOISÉS KAUFMAN. Today the company tried to explain to me to no avail what chicken fried steak was.

WAITRESS. "Now, are you from Wyoming? Or are you just passing through?"

LEIGH FONDAKOWSKI. "We're just passing through."

NARRATOR. Company member Barbara Pitts.

BARBARA PITTS. We arrived in Laramie tonight. Just past the "Welcome to Laramie" sign — "Population 26,687" — the first thing to greet us was Walmart. In the dark, we could be on any

27

main drag in America — fast food chains, gas stations. But as we drove into the downtown area by the railroad tracks, the buildings still looked like a turn-of-the-century Western town. Oh, and as we passed the University Inn, on the sign where amenities such as heated pool or cable TV are usually touted, it said. HATE IS NOT A LARAMIE VALUE.

NARRATOR. Greg Pierotti.

MOMENT: ALISON AND MARGE

GREG PIEROTTI. I met today with two long-time Laramie residents, Alison Mears and Marge Murray. Two social service workers who taught me a thing or two.

ALISON MEARS. Well, what Laramie used to be like when Marge was growing up, well, it was mostly rural.

MARGE MURRAY. Yeah, it was. I enjoyed it, you know. My kids all had horses.

ALISON MEARS. Well, there was more land. I mean, you could keep your pet cow. Your horse. Your little chickens. You know, just have your little bit of acreage.

MARGE MURRAY. Yeah, I could run around the house in my all togethers, do the housework while the kids were in school. And nobody could see me. And if they got that close …

ALISON MEARS. Well, then that's their problem.

MARGE MURRAY. Yeah.

GREG PIEROTTI. I just want to make sure I got the expression right, in your all togethers?

MARGE MURRAY. Well, yeah, honey, why wear clothes?

ALISON MEARS. Now, how's he gonna use that in his play?

GREG PIEROTTI. So this was a big ranching town?

ALISON MEARS. Oh, not just ranching, this was a big railroad town at one time. Before they moved everything to Cheyenne and Green River and Omaha. So now well, it's just a drive through spot for the railroad — because even what was it, in the fifties? Well, they had one big roundhouse, and they had such a shop they could build a complete engine.

MARGE MURRAY. They did. My mom worked there.

GREG PIEROTTI. Your mom worked in a roundhouse?

MARGE MURRAY. Yep. She washed engines. Her name was Minnie. We used to, you know, sing that song for her. You know that song.

GREG PIEROTTI. What song?

MARGE MURRAY. "Run for the roundhouse. Minnie. They can't corner you there." *(They crack up.)*

ALISON MEARS. But I'll tell you, Wyoming is bad in term of jobs. I mean, the University has the big high whoop-dee-doo jobs. But Wyoming, unless you're a professional, well, the bulk of the people are working minimum wage jobs.

MARGE MURRAY. Yeah, I've been either in the service industry or bartending most of my life. Now I know everybody in town.

ALISON MEARS. And she does.

MARGE MURRAY. And I do. Now that I'll tell ya, here in Laramie there is a difference and there always has been. What it is is a class distinction. It's about the well educated and the ones that are not. And the educated don't understand why the ones that are not don't get educated. That's why I told you before my kids had to fight because their mother was a bartender. Never mind I was the best damn bartender in town.

ALISON MEARS. And she was.

MARGE MURRAY. That's not bragging, that's fact.

ALISON MEARS. But here in Laramie, if it weren't for the University, we'd just be S.O.L.

GREG PIEROTTI. What's S.O.L.?

ALISON MEARS. Well, do I have to say it? Well, it's shit outta luck. *(She cracks up.)* Oh Lordy, you've got that on your tape. Boy, you are getting an education today.

GREG PIEROTTI. Yeah, I guess I am. So, let me just ask you — what was your response when this happened to Matthew Shepard?

MARGE MURRAY. Well, I've been close enough to the case to know many of the people. I have a daughter that's on the sheriff's department.

As far as the gay issue, I don't give a damn one way or the other as long as they don't bother me. And even if they did, I'd just say no thank you. And that's the attitude of most of the Laramie population. They might poke one, if they were in a bar situation you know, they had been drinking, they might actually smack one in the mouth, but then they'd just walk away. Most of 'em said they would just say, "I don't swing that way," and whistle on about their business. Laramie is live and let live.

ALISON MEARS. I'd say that Marge probably knows a lot more except she's even willing to say and we have to respect her for that.

MARGE MURRAY. Well, uh, where are you going with this story?

GREG PIEROTTI. Oh well, we still haven't decided. When we've finished, we are going to try to bring it around to Laramie.

MARGE MURRAY. Okay, then, there are parts I won't tell you.

MOMENT: MATTHEW

NARRATOR. Company member Andy Paris.

ANDY PARIS: Today for the first time, we met someone who actually knew Matthew Shepard. Trish Steger, owner of a shop in town, referred to him as "Matt."

TRISH STEGER. Matt used to come into my shop —- that's how I knew him.

ANDY PARIS. It was the first time I heard him referred to as Matt instead of Matthew. "Did he go by Matt to everyone?"

DOC O'CONNOR: Well, on the second of October, I get a phone call about, uh, ten after seven.

NARRATOR. Doc O'Connor.

DOC O'CONNOR. It was Matthew Shepard. And he said, "Can you pick me up at the corner of Third and Grand?" So, anyhow, I pull up to the corner, to see who Matthew Shepard, you know. It's a little guy, about five-two, soakin' wet, I betcha ninety-seven pounds tops. They say he weighed a hundred and ten, but I wouldn't believe it. They also said he was five-five in the newspapers, but this man he was really only about five-two, maybe five-one. So he walks up the window — I'm gonna try and go in steps

30

so you can better understand the principle of this man. So he walks up to the window, and I say, "Are you Matthew Shepard?" And he says, "Yeah, I'm Matthew Shepard. But, I don't want you to call me Matthew, or Mr. Shepard. I don't want you to call me anything. My name is Matt. And I want you to know, I am gay and we're going to go to a gay bar. Do you have a problem with that?" And I said, "How're you payin'?"

The fact is ... Laramie doesn't have any gay bars ... and for that matter neither does Wyoming ... so he was hiring me to take him down to Fort Collins, Colorado, about an hour away.

Matt was a blunt little shit, you know what I'm sayin'? — he always was. But I liked him 'cause he was straightforward, you see what I'm saying? Maybe gay but straightforward, you see what I'm saying?

TRISH STEGER. I don't know, you know, how does any one person ever tell about another? You really should talk to my sister Romaine. She was a very close friend of Matthew's.

ROMAINE PATTERSON. We never called him Matthew actually. Most of the time we called him "Choo-choo." You know, because we used to call him Mattchew, and then we just called him Choo-choo.

And whenever I think of Matthew, I always think of his incredible beaming smile. I mean, he'd walk in and he'd be like, *(Demonstrates.)* you know, and he'd smile at everyone ... he just made you feel great ... And he — would like stare people down in the coffee shop ... 'cause he always wanted to sit on the end seat so that he could talk to me while I was working. And if someone was sitting in that seat, he would just sit there and stare at them. Until they left. And then he would claim his spot.

But Matthew definitely had a political side to him ... I mean, he really wanted to get into political affairs ... that's all his big interest was, was watching CNN and MSNBC, I mean, that's the only TV station I ever saw his TV tuned into. He was just really smart in political affairs, but not too smart on like common sense things ...

So, he moves to Laramie to go to school.

JON PEACOCK. Matthew was very shy when he first came in.

NARRATOR. Jon Peacock, Matthew Shepard's academic adviser.

JON PEACOCK. To the point of being somewhat mousy, I'd almost say. He was having some difficulties adjusting, but this was home for him and he made that quite clear. And, so his mousyness, his shyness gave way to a person who was excited about this track that he was going to embark on. He was just figuring out wanting to work on human rights, how he was going to do that. And when that happens this person begins to bloom a little bit. He was starting to say, "Wow, there are opportunities here. There are things I can do in this world. I can be important."

ROMAINE PATTERSON. I did hear from Matthew about forty-eight hours before his attack. And he told me that he had joined the gay and lesbian group on campus, and he said he was enjoying it. You know, he was getting ready for Pride Week and what not. I mean, he was totally stoked about school — yeah, he was really happy about being there.

JON PEACOCK. And in retrospect and I can only say this in retrospect, of course, I think that's where he was heading, towards human rights. Which only adds to the irony and tragedy of this.

MOMENT: WHO'S GETTING WHAT?

DOC O'CONNOR. Let me tell you something else here, There's more gay people in Wyoming than meets the eye. I know, I know for a fact. They're not particularly, ah, the whatta you call them, the queens, the gay people, queens, you know, run around faggot type people. No, they're the ones that throw bail, hay, jump on horses, brand 'em and kick ass, you see what I'm saying? As I always say, don't fuck with a Wyoming queer, 'cause they will kick you in your fucking ass, but that's not the point of what I'm trying to say. 'Cause I know a lot of gay people in Wyoming. I know a lot of people period. I've been lived up here some forty-odd years, you see what I'm saying?

And I don't think Wyoming people give a damn one way or another if you're gay or straight, that's just what I just said, doesn't matter. If there's eight men and one woman in a Wyoming bar which is often the case, now you stop and think — who's getting what? You see what I'm saying? Now jeez, it don't take a big intelligent mind to figure that one out.

MOMENT: EASIER SAID THAN DONE

CATHERINE CONNOLLY. My understanding when I first came here …
NARRATOR. Catherine Connolly.
CATHERINE CONNOLLY. … is that I was the first "out" lesbian or gay faculty member on campus. And that was in 1992. So, that wasn't that long ago. Um, I was asked at my interview what my husband did, um, and so I came out then … Do you want a funny story?

When you first get here as a new faculty member, there's all these things you have to do. And so, I was in my office and I noticed that this woman called … I was expecting, you know, it was a health-insurance phone call, something like that, and so I called her back. And I could hear her. She's working on her keyboard, clicking away — I said, you know, "This is Cathy Connolly returning your phone call." And she said, "Oh. It's you." And I thought, "This is bizarre." And she said, "I hear — I hear — I hear you're gay. I hear you are." I was like, "Uh huh." And she said, "I hear you came as a couple. I'm one too. Not a couple, just a person." And so — she was — a kind of lesbian who knew I was coming and she wanted to come over and meet me immediately. And she later told me that there were other lesbians that she knew who wouldn't be seen with me. That I would irreparably taint them, that just to be seen with me could be a problem.
JONAS SLONAKER. When I came here I knew it was going to be hard as a gay man.
NARRATOR. Jonas Slonaker.
JONAS SLONAKER. But I kept telling myself, people should live where they want to live. And there would be times I would to go down to Denver and I would go to gay bars and, um, people

would ask where I was from and I'd say, "Laramie, Wyoming." And I met so many men down there from Wyoming. So many gay men who grew up here and they're like, this is not a place where I can live, how can you live there, I had to get out, grrr, grrr, grrr. But every once in a while there would be a guy, "Oh gosh, I miss Laramie. I mean, I really love it there, that's where I want to live. And they get this starry-eyed look and I'm like, if that's where you want to live, do it. I mean, imagine if more gay people stayed in small towns ... But it's easier said than done, of course.

MOMENT: JOURNAL ENTRIES

MOISÉS KAUFMAN. Today we are moving from our motel and heading for the Best Western.
NARRATOR. Moisés Kaufman.
MOISÉS KAUFMAN. My hope is that it is a better Western.
NARRATOR. Amanda Gronich.
AMANDA GRONICH. Today we divided up to go to different churches in the community. Moisés and I were given a Baptist Church. We were welcomed into the services by the Reverend himself standing at the entrance to the chapel. This is what I remember of his sermon that morning.

MOMENT: THE WORD

BAPTIST MINISTER. My dear brothers and sisters. I am here today to bring you the Word of the Lord. Now, I have a simple truth that I tell to my colleagues and I'm gonna tell it to you today. The word is either sufficient or it is not.

Scientists tell me that human history, that the world is five billion or six billion years old — after all, what's a billion years, give or take. The Bible tells me that human history is 6,000 years old.

The word is either sufficient or it is not.

STEPHEN MEAD JOHNSON. Ah, the sociology of religion in the West ...

NARRATOR. Stephen Mead Johnson, Unitarian Minister.

STEPHEN MEAD JOHNSON. Dominant religious traditions in this town. Baptist, Mormon — they're everywhere, it's not just Salt Lake, you know, they're all over — they're like jam on toast down here.

DOUG LAWS. The Mormon Church has a little different thing going that irritates some folks.

NARRATOR. Doug Laws, Stake Ecclesiastical Leader for the Mormon Church.

DOUG LAWS. And that is that we absolutely believe that God still speaks to man. We don't think that it happened and some folks wrote it in the Bible. God speaks to us today, and we believe that. We believe that the prophet of the church has the authority to receive inspiration and revelation from God.

STEPHEN MEAD JOHNSON. So, the spectrum would be — uh, on the left side of that panel, so far left that I am probably sitting by myself, is me — and the Unitarian Church. Unitarians are by and large humanists, many of whom are atheists, I mean — we're, you know, we're not even sure we're a religion. And to my right on the spectrum, to his credit, Father Roger, Catholic Priest, who is well established here, and God bless him —- he did not equivocate at all when this happened — he hosted the vigil for Matthew that night.

FATHER ROGER SCHMIT. I was really jolted because, you know, when we did the vigil — we wanted to get other ministers involved and we called some of them, and they were not going to get involved. And it was like, "We are gonna stand back and wait and see which way the wind is blowing." And that angered me immensely. We are supposed to stand out as leaders. I thought, "Wow, what's going on here?"

DOUG LAWS. God has set boundaries. And one of our responsibilities is to learn. What is it that God wants? So you study scripture, you look to your leaders. Then you know what the bounds are. Now once you kinda know what the bounds are, then you sorta get a feel for what's out of bounds.

There is a proclamation that came out on the family. A family is defined as one woman and one man and children. That's a family. That's about as clear as you can state it. There's no sexual deviation in the Morman Church. No — no leniency. We just think it's out of bounds.

BAPTIST MINISTER. I warn you, you will be mocked! You will be ridiculed for the singularity of your faith! But you let the Bible be your guide. It's in there. It's all in there.

STEPHEN MEAD JOHNSON. The Christian pastors, many of the conservative ones, were silent on this. Conservative Christians use the Bible to show the rest of the world it says here in the Bible. And most Americans believe, and they do, that the Bible is the word of God, and how you gonna fight that?

BAPTIST MINISTER. I am a Biblicist. Which means, the Bible doesn't need ME to be true. The Bible is true whether I believe it or not. The word is either sufficient or it is not!

STEPHEN MEAD JOHNSON. I arrived in Laramie on September fifteenth. I looked around — tumbleweed, cement factory — and said, "What in the hell am I doing in Wyoming?" Three weeks later, I found out what the hell I'm doing in Wyoming.

MOMENT: A SCARF

STEPHEN BELBER. I had breakfast this morning with a University student named Zubaida Ula. She is an Islamic Feminist who likes to do things her own way.

ZUBAIDA ULA. I've lived in Laramie since I was four. Yeah. My parents are from Bangladesh. Two years ago, because I'm Muslim, I decided to start wearing a scarf. That's really changed my life in Laramie. Yeah.

Like people say things to me like, "Why do you have to wear that thing on your head?" Like when I go to the grocery store, I'm not looking to give people Islam 101, you know what I mean? So I'll be like, well, it's part of my religion and they'll be — this is the worst part 'cuz they'll be like, "I know it's part of your religion, but why?" And it's — how am I supposed to go into the whole doctrine of physical modesty and my own spiritual relationship with the Lord, standing there with my pop and chips? You know what I mean?

STEPHEN BELBER. Yeah.

ZUBAIDA ULA. You know, it's so unreal to me that, yeah, that a group from New York would be writing a play about Laramie. And then I was picturing like you're gonna be in a play about my town. You're gonna be onstage in New York and you're gonna be acting like you're us. That's so weird.

MOMENT: LIFESTYLE 1

MINISTER'S WIFE. Hello?

AMANDA GRONICH. Yes, hello. My name is Amanda Gronich and I am here in Laramie working with a theater company. I went to the Reverend's, your husband's church on Sunday, and I was extremely interested in talking with the Reverend about some of his thoughts about recent events.

MINISTER'S WIFE. Well, I don't think he'll want to talk to you. He has very Biblical views about homosexuality — he doesn't condone that kind of violence. But he doesn't condone that kind of lifestyle, you know what I mean? And he was just bombarded with press after this happened and the media has been just terrible about this whole thing.

AMANDA GRONICH. Oh, I know, I really understand. It must have just been terrible.

MINISTER'S WIFE. Oh, yes, I think we are all hoping this just goes away.

AMANDA GRONICH. Well, um do you think maybe I could call back and speak with your husband just briefly?

MINISTER'S WIFE. Well, all right you can call him back tonight at nine o'clock.

AMANDA GRONICH. Oh, thank you so much. I'll do that.

MOMENT: THE FIRESIDE

STEPHEN BELBER. Today Barbara and I went to the Fireside Bar, which is the last place Matthew was seen in public.

BARBARA PITTS. The Fireside — definitely feels like a college bar, with a couple of pool tables and a stage area for karaoke night. Still the few regulars in the late afternoon were hardly the college crowd.

STEPHEN BELBER. First person we talked to was Matt Mickelson, the owner.

MATT MICKELSON. My great-great grandfather moved here in 1862. He owned Laramie's first opera house. It was called Old Blue Front, and in 1870 Louisa Grandma Swain cast the first woman's ballot in any free election in the world, and that's why Wyoming is the Equality State, so what I want to do is reestablish my bar business as Old Blue Front Opera House and Good Time Emporium. You know, I want to have a restaurant. I want to have a gift shop. I want to have a pool hall and do all this shit, you know ... Every night's ladies night ...

So the Fireside is the first step towards the Old Blue Front Opera house and Good Time Emporium.

BARBARA PITTS. So, what about the night Matthew Shepard was here?

MATT MICKELSON. We had karaoke that night, twenty or thirty people here — Matthew Shepard came in, sitting right — right where you're sitting, just hanging out ... I mean, if you wanna talk to somebody, you should talk to Matt Galloway. He was the kid that was bartending that night. You'd have to meet him. His character stands for itself. *(Calling.)* HEY, IS GALLOWAY BARTENDING TONIGHT?

MATT GALLOWAY. Okay. I'm gonna make this brief, quick, get it over with, but it will be everything — factual. Just the facts. Here we go. Ten o'clock. I clock in, usual time, Tuesday nights. ten-thirty — Matthew Shepard shows up — alone, sits down, orders a Heineken.

NARRATOR. Phil Labrie, friend of Matthew Shepard

PHIL LABRIE. Matt liked to drink Heineken and nothing else. Heineken even though you have to pay nine-fifty for a six pack. He'd always buy the same beer.

MATT GALLOWAY. So what can I tell you about Matt?

If you had a hundred customers like him it'd be the — the most perfect bar I've ever been in. Okay? And nothing to do with sexual orientation. Um, absolute mannerisms. Manners. Politeness, intelligence.

Taking care of me, as in tips. Everything — conversation, uh, dressed nice, clean cut. Some people you just know, sits down, "Please," "Thank you," — offers intellect, you know, within — within — within their vocabulary.

Um, so, he kicks it there. Didn't seem to have any worries, or like he was looking for anyone. Just enjoy his drink and the company around.

Now approximately eleven forty-five, eleven-thirty — eleven forty-five, Aaron McKinney and Russell Henderson come in — I didn't know their names then, but they're the accused. They're the perps, they're the accused. They walked in, just very stone-faced, you know. Dirty. Grungy. Rude. "Gimme." That type of thing. They walked up to the bar, uh, and as you know, paid for a pitcher with dimes and quarters, uh, which is something that I mean you don't forget. You don't forget that. Five-fifty in dimes and quarters. That's a freakin' nightmare.

Now Henderson and McKinney — they didn't seem intoxificated at all. They came in — they just ordered a beer, took the pitcher with them back there into the poolroom, and kept to themselves. Next thing I knew, probably a half hour later, they were kind of walking around — no beer. And I remember thinking to myself that I'm not gonna ask them if they want another one, because obviously they just paid for a pitcher with dimes and quarters, I have a real good feeling they don't have any more money.

NARRATOR. Romaine Patterson.

ROMAINE PATTERSON. Money meant nothing to Matthew, because he came from a lot of it. And he would like hand over his wallet in two seconds — because money meant nothing. His —

shoes — might have meant something. They can say it was robbery … I don't buy it. For even an iota of a second.

MATT GALLOWAY. Then a few moments later I looked over and Aaron and Russell had been talking to Matthew Shepard.

KRISTIN PRICE. Aaron said that a guy walked up to him and said that he was gay and wanted to get with Aaron and Russ.

NARRATOR Kristin Price, girlfriend of Aaron McKinney

KRISTIN PRICE. And that he got aggravated with it and told him that he was straight and didn't want anything to do with him and walked off. He said that is when he and Russell went to the bathroom and decided to pretend they were gay and get him in the truck and rob him.

MATT GALLOWAY. Okay, no. They stated that Matt approached them, that he came onto them. I absolutely, positively disbelieve and refute the statement one hundred percent. Refute it. I'm gonna give you two reasons why.

One. Character reference. Why would he approach them? Why them? He wasn't approaching anybody else in the bar. They say he's gay, he was a flaming gay, he's gonna come on to people like that. Bullshit. He never came on to me. Hello?!? He came on to them? I don't believe it.

Two. Territorialism. Is — is — is the word I will use for this. And that's the fact that Matt was sitting there. Russell and Aaron were in the pool area. Upon their first interaction, they were in Matt's area, in the area that Matt had been seen all night. So who approached who by that?

ROMAINE PATTERSON. But Matthew was the kind of person … like, he would never not talk to someone for any reason. If someone started talking to him, he'd just be like, "Oh, blah, blah, blah." He never had any problem just striking up a conversation with ANYBODY.

PHIL LABRIE. Matt did feel lonely a lot of times. Me knowing that — and knowing how gullible Matt could be … he would have walked right into it. The fact that he was at the bar alone without any friends made him that much more vulnerable.

MATT GALLOWAY. So the only thing is — and this is what I'm testifying to — 'cause you know, I'm also, basically, the key eyewitness in this case, uh … *(Pause.)* Basically what I'm testifying is

40

that I saw Matthew leave. I saw two individuals leave with Matthew. I didn't see their faces, but I saw the back of their heads. At the same time, McKinney and Henderson were no longer around. You do the math.

MATT MICKELSON. Actually, I think the DJ was the last one to talk to him on his way out that night … gave him a cigarette or something. His name is Shadow.

SHADOW. I was the last person that Matt talked to before he left the Fireside … I was just bullshittin' around with my shit, and he stopped me. I stopped him actually, and he's like, "Hey, Shadow," da da da, and I was like, "What, man, you gettin' ready to leave?" He's like, "Yeah man," and this an' that. But then I noticed them two guys and they stood outside. You could see, you could see it. They were standing there, you know, and he was looking over to them, and they were lookin' back at him. And I stood and talked to Matt for like a good ten minutes and you seen the guys with him, you seen 'em getting like, you seen 'em like worried, like, you know, anxious to leave and shit — So when they took off, I seen it, when they took off. It was in a black truck, it was a small truck, and the three of them sat in the front seat and Matt sat in the middle.

And I didn't think nothin' of it, you know. I didn't figure them guys was gonna be like that.

MOMENT: MCKINNEY AND HENDERSON

NARRATOR. A friend of Aaron McKinney.

ANONYMOUS. Oh, I've known Aaron a long time. Aaron was a good kid. I liked Aaron a lot. That's why I was shocked when I heard this. I'm like … I know he was, he was living out far … at his trailer house is what he told me, with his girl … They just started dating last summer … They musta gotten pregnant as soon as they started dating, you know, 'cause they had a kid. He was only twenty-one years old, but he was running around with a kid … You see that's the kinda person Aaron was, just like he always dressed in like big clothes, you know like, in like Tommy "Hile-

41

Figer," Polo, Gucci ...

At the time I knew him, he was just, he was just a young kid trying to, you know, he just wanted to fit in, you know, acting tough, acting cool, but, you know, you could get in his face about it and he would back down, like he was some kinda scared kid.

NARRATOR. Sherry Aanenson.

SHERRY AANENSON. Russell was just so sweet. He was the one who was the Eagle Scout. I mean his whole presence was just quiet and sweet. So, of course, it doesn't make sense to me and I know people snap and whatever and like it wasn't a real intimate relationship. I was just his landlord. I did work with him at the Chuck Wagon too. And I remember like at the Christmas party he was just totally drunk out of his mind, like we all were pretty much just party party time ... And he wasn't belligerent. He didn't change, his personality didn't change. He was still the same little meek Russell. I remember him coming up to me and saying "When you get a chance Sherry, can I have a dance?" Which we never did get around to doing that, but ... Now I just want to shake him, you know, what were you thinking? What in the hell were you thinking?

MOMENT: THE FENCE

STEPHEN MEAD JOHNSON. The fence — I've been out there four times. I've taken visitors. That place has become a pilgrimage site. Clearly that's a very powerful personal experience to go out there. It is so stark and so empty and you can't help but think of Matthew there for eighteen hours in nearly freezing temperatures, with that view up there isolated, and, the "God, my God, why have you forsaken me?" comes to mind.

NARRATOR. Company Member Greg Pierotti.

GREG PIEROTTI. Phil Labrie, a friend of Matthew's, took us to the fence this morning. I broke down the minute I touched it. I feel such a strong kinship with this young man. On the way back, I made sure that no one saw me crying.

42

NARRATOR. Leigh Fondakowski.

LEIGH FONDAKOWSKI. Greg was crying on the way back. I couldn't bring myself to tears, but I felt the same way. I have an interview this afternoon with Aaron Kreifels. He's the boy who found Matthew out there at the fence. I don't think I'm up for it right now. I'll see if someone else can do it.

MOMENT: FINDING MATTHEW SHEPARD

AARON KREIFELS. Well I, uh, I took off on my bicycle about five o'clock P.M. on Wednesday from my dorm. I just kinda felt like going for a ride. So I —— I went up to the top of Cactus Canyon, and I'm not super familiar with that area, so on my way back down, I didn't know where I was going. I was just sort of picking the way to go, which now … it just makes me think that God wanted me to find him because there's no way that I was going to go that way.

So I was in some deep ass sand, and I wanted to turn around —- but for some reason, I kept going. And, uh, I went along, And there was this rock on the —— on the ground —— and I just drilled it. I went —— over the handlebars and ended up on the ground.

So, uh, I got up, and I was just kind of dusting myself off, and I was looking around and I noticed something —— which ended up to be Matt, and he was just lying there by a fence, and I —— I just thought it was a scarecrow. I was like, Halloween's coming up, thought it was a Halloween gag, so I didn't think much of it, so I got my bike, walked it around the fence that was there. It was a buck type fence. And, uh, got closer to him and I noticed his hair —- and that was a major key to me, noticing it was a human being —- was his hair. 'Cause I just thought it was a dummy, seriously, I noticed —— I even noticed the chest going up and down. I still thought it was a dummy, you know. I thought it was just like some kind of mechanism.

But when I saw hair, well, I knew it was a human being.

So … I ran to the nearest house and —— I just ran as fast as I

43

could … and called the police.

REGGIE FLUTY. I responded to the call.

NARRATOR. Officer Reggie Fluty.

REGGIE FLUTY. When I got there, the first — at first the only thing I could see was partially somebody's feet and I got out of my vehicle and raced over — I seen what appeared to be a young man, thirteen, fourteen years old, because he was so tiny, laying on his back and he was tied to the bottom end of a pole.

I did the best I could. The gentleman that was laying on the ground, Matthew Shepard, he was covered in dry blood all over his head. There was dry blood underneath him and he was barely breathing … he was doing the best he could.

I was going to breath for him and I couldn't get his mouth open — his mouth wouldn't open for me.

He was covered in, like I said, partially dry blood and blood all over his head — the only place that he did not have any blood on him, on his face, was what appeared to be where he had been crying down his face.

His head was distorted. You know, it did not look normal — he looked as if he had a real harsh head wound.

DR. CANTWAY. I was working the emergency room the night Matthew Shepard was brought in. I don't think, that any of us, ah, can remember seeing a patient in that condition for a long time — those of us who've worked in big city hospitals have seen this. Ah, but we have some people here who've not worked in a big city hospital. And, ah, it's not something you expect here.

Ah, you expect it, you expect this kind of injuries to come from a car going down a hill at eighty miles an hour. You expect to see gross injuries from something like that — this horrendous, terrible thing. Ah, but you don't expect to see that from someone doing this to another person.

The ambulance report said it was a beating so we knew.

AARON KREIFELS. There was nothing I could do. I mean, if there was anything that I could've done to help him, I would've done it, but there was nothing.

And I, I was yelling at the top of my lungs at him, trying to get something outta him.

Like, "Hey, wake up!" "HELLO!"

44

But he didn't move, he didn't flinch, he didn't anything ...

REGGIE FLUTY. He was tied to the fence — his hands were thumbs out in what we call a cuffing position — the way we handcuff people. He was bound with a real thin white rope. It went around the bottom of the pole, about four inches up off the ground.

His shoes were missing.

He was tied extremely tight — so I used my boot knife and tried to slip it between the rope and his wrist — I had to be extremely careful not to harm Matthew any further.

DR. CANTWAY. Your first thought is ... well certainly you'd like to think that it's somebody from out of town, that comes through and beats somebody. I mean, things like this happen, you know, shit happens, and it happens in Laramie. But if there's been somebody who has been beaten repeatedly, ah, certainly this is something that offends us. I think that's a good word. It offends us!

REGGIE FLUTY. He was bound so tight — I finally got the knife through there — I'm sorry — we rolled him over to his left side — when we did that he quit breathing. Immediately, I put him back on his back — and that was just enough of an adjustment — it gave me enough room to cut him free there.

I seen the EMS unit trying to get to the location. Once the ambulance got there we put a neck collar on him, placed him on a back board and scooted him from underneath the fence — then Rob drove the ambulance to Ivinson Hospital's Emergency Room ...

DR. CANTWAY. Now, the strange thing is, twenty minutes before Matthew came in, Aaron McKinney was brought in by his girlfriend. Now I guess he had gotten into a fight later on that night back in town, so I am workin' on Aaron and the ambulance comes in with Matthew. Now at this point I don't know that there's a connection — at all. So I tell Aaron to wait and I go and treat Matthew. So there's Aaron in one room of the ER and Matthew in another room two doors down.

Now as soon as we saw Matthew ... It was very obvious that his care was beyond our capabilities. Called the neurosurgeon at Poudre Valley, and he was on the road in an hour and fifteen minutes, I think.

REGGIE FLUTY. They showed me a picture ... days later I saw

a picture of Matthew ... I would have never recognized him.

DR. CANTWAY. Then two days later I found out the connection and I was ... very ... struck!!! They were two kids!!!!! They were both my patients and they were two kids. I took care of both of them ... of both their bodies. And ... for a brief moment I wondered if this is how God feels when he looks down at us. How we are all his kids ... Our bodies ... Our souls ... And I felt a great deal of compassion ... for both of them ...

End of Act One

ACT TWO

MOMENT: A LARAMIE MAN

NARRATOR. This is Jon Peacock, Matthew's academic adviser.

JON PEACOCK. Well, the news reports started trickling out on Thursday, but no names were mentioned. The brutality of the crime was not mentioned. All that was mentioned was that there was a man, Laramie man, found beaten, out on the prairie basically. Later on in the evening they mentioned his name. It was like that can't, that's not the Matthew Shepard I know. That's not my student. That's not this person who I've been meeting with.

ROMAINE PATTERSON. I was in the coffee shop.

NARRATOR. Romaine Patterson.

ROMAINE PATTERSON. And someone pulled me aside and said, "I don't know much, but they say that there's been a young man who's been beaten in Laramie. And they said his name was Matthew Shepard." And he said, "Do you think this could be our Matthew?"

And I said, "Well, yeah, it sounds like it could be our Matthew."

So I called up my sister Trish and I said, "Tell me what you know." I'm just like — "I need to know anything you know because I don't know anything."

TRISH STEGER. So I'm talking to my sister on the phone and that's when the whole story came up on Channel 5 news and it was just like "baboom."

JON PEACOCK. And the news reports kept rolling in, young University of Wyoming student, his age, his description, it's like, "Oh my God."

TRISH STEGER. And, uh ... *(Pause.)* I — I felt sick to my stomach ... it's just instantly sick to my stomach. And I had to tell Romaine, "Yes, it was Matthew. It was your friend."

MATT GALLOWAY. Well, I'll tell you — I'll tell you what is

overwhelming.

NARRATOR. Matt Galloway

MATT GALLOWAY. Friday morning I first find out about it. I go to class, walk out, "boom" there it is — in the *Branding Iron.* So immediately I drive to the nearest newsstand, buy a *Laramie Boomerang* 'cause I want more details, buy that — go home ... before I can even open the paper, my boss calls me, he says:

MATT MICKELSON. "Did you hear about what happened?"

MATT GALLOWAY. I'm like, "Yeah."

MATT MICKELSON. "Was he in the bar Tuesday night?"

MATT GALLOWAY. I go, "Yes, yes he was."

MATT MICKELSON. "You've got to get down to the bar right now. We've got to talk about this. We've got to discuss what's going to go on."

JON PEACOCK. By this time, I was starting to get upset, but still the severity wasn't out yet.

RULON STACEY. It was Thursday afternoon.

NARRATOR. Rulon Stacey at Poudre Valley Hospital.

RULON STACEY. I got a call. "We just got a kid in from Wyoming and it looks like he may be the victim of a hate crime. We have a couple of newspaper reporters here asking questions." And so, we agreed that we needed one spokesperson. As CEO, I'll do that and we'll try and gather all the information that we can.

ROMAINE PATTERSON. And then I watched the ten o'clock news that night, where they started speaking about the nature and the seriousness of it ...

MATT GALLOWAY. So I'm on the phone with Michelson and he's like:

MATT MICKELSON. We need to go to the arraignment so we can identify these guys and make sure these guys were in the bar.

MATT GALLOWAY. So we go to the arraignment.

MOMENT: THE ESSENTIAL FACTS

NEWSPERSON. Our focus today turns to Laramie, Wyoming, and the Albany County Courthouse, where Aaron James McKinney and Russell Arthur Henderson are being charged for the brutal beating of Matthew Shepard, a gay University of Wyoming student.

CATHERINE CONNOLLY. The arraignment was on Friday. Right around lunch time. And I said, "I'm just going." I just took off — it's just down the street. So I walked a few blocks and I went. Has anybody told you about the arraignment?

There were probably about a hundred people from town and probably as many news media by that point. A lot more of the details had come out. The fact that the perpetrators were kids themselves, local kids, that everyone who's from around here has some relationship to. And what — everyone was really, I think, waiting on pins and needles for what would happen when the perpetrators walked in. And what happened — there's 200 people in the room at this point ... They walked in in their complete orange jumpsuits and their shackles, and you could have heard a pin drop.

It was incredibly solemn.

I mean, lots of people were teary at that point. Then the judge came in and did a reading — there was a reading of the evidence that the prosecution has and — it's just a — it's a statement of facts and the reading of the facts was ...

JUDGE. The essential facts are that the defendants, Aaron James and McKinney and Russell Arthur Henderson, met Matthew Shepard at the Fireside Bar, and after Mr. Shepard confided he was gay, the subjects deceived Mr. Shepard into leaving with them in their vehicle to a remote area. Upon arrival at said area, both subjects tied their victim to a buck fence, robbed him, tortured him, and beat him ... Both defendants were later contacted by officers of the Laramie Police Department who observed inside the cab of their pickup, a credit card and a pair of black patent leather shoes belonging to the victim, Matthew Shepard. *(The Judge goes sotto voce here while Catherine Connolly speaks.)* The subjects took the victim's credit card, wallet containing twenty dollars in cash, his shoes, and other items, and obtained the victim's address in order to later burglarize his home.

CATHERINE CONNOLLY. I don't think there was any person who was left in that courtroom who wasn't crying at the end of it. I mean it lasted — five minutes, but it kept on getting more and more horrific, ending with:

JUDGE. Said defendants left the victim begging for his life.

MOMENT: LIVE AND LET LIVE

NARRATOR. Sergeant Hing.

SGT. HING. How could this happen? I — I think a lot of people just don't understand, and even I don't really understand, how someone can do something like that. We have one of the most vocal populations of gay people in the state ... And it's pretty much. Live and let live.

NARRATOR. Laramie resident Jeffrey Lockwood.

JEFFREY LOCKWOOD. My secret hope was that they were from somewhere else, that then of course you can create that distance. We don't grow children like that here. Well, it's pretty clear that we do grow children like that here ...

CATHERINE CONNOLLY. So that was the arraignment and my response — was pretty catatonic — not sleeping, not eating. Don't — you know, don't leave me alone right now.

JON PEACOCK. More and more details came in about the sheer brutality, um, motivations, how this happened. And then quite frankly the media descended and there was no time to reflect on it anymore.

MOMENT: THE GEM CITY OF THE PLAINS

Many newspeople enter the stage followed by technical crews carrying video cameras, microphones and media lights. The newspeople begin to speak into the cameras. Simultaneously, television monitors enter the space — in our production they flew in from above the light grid. In the monitors, one can see in live feed the newspeople onstage as well as other media images. The reporters' texts overlap to create a kind of media cacophony. This moment should feel like an invasion and should be so perceived by the other actors onstage.

NEWSPERSON #1. Laramie, Wyoming — often called the "gem city of the plains" is now at the eye of the storm. *(Enter Newsperson #2 — Newsperson #1 goes sotto voce.)* The cowboy state has its rednecks and yahoos, for sure, but there are no more bigots per capita in Wyoming than there are in New York, Florida or California. The difference is that in Wyoming there are fewer places to blend in if you're anything other than prairie stock

NEWSPERSON #2. Aaron McKinney and his friend Russell Henderson came from the poor side of town. *(Enter Newsperson #3 — Newsperson #2 goes sotto voce.)* Both were from broken homes and as teenagers had had run-ins with the law. They lived in trailer parks and scratched out a living working at fast-food restaurants and fixing roofs.

NEWSPERSON #3. As a gay college student lay hospitalized in critical condition after a severe beating *(Enter Newsperson #4 — Newsperson #3 goes sotto voce.)* this small city, which bills itself as "Wyoming's hometown," wrestled with its attitudes toward gay men.

NEWSPERSON #4. People would like to think that what happened to Matthew was an exception to the rule, but it was an extreme version of what happens in our schools on a daily basis. *(The voices and sounds have escalated to a high pitch. And the last text we hear is:)*

51

NEWSPERSON #1. It's a tough business, as Matt Shepard knew, and as his friends all know, to be gay in cowboy country. *(These reporters continue speaking into the cameras sotto voce over the next texts.)*

JON PEACOCK. It was huge. Yeah. It was herds and — and we're talking hundreds of reporters which makes a huge dent in this town's population. There's reporters everywhere, news trucks everywhere on campus, everywhere in the town. And we're not used to that type of attention to begin with. We're not used to that type of exposure.

NARRATOR. Tiffany Edwards, local reporter.

TIFFANY EDWARDS. These people are predators. Like this one journalist actually caught one of the judges in the bathroom at the urinal and was like asking him questions. And the judge was like, "Excuse me, can I please have some privacy?" And the journalist was like OFFENDED that he asked for privacy. I mean, this is not how journalism started, like the Gutenberg Press, you know.

DOC O'CONNOR. I'll tell you what, when *Hardcopy* came and taped me, I taped them at the exact same time. I have every word I ever said on tape, so if they ever do anything funny they better watch their fuckin' ass.

NEWSPERSON. Wyoming Governor Jim Geringer, a first-term Republican up for reelection.

GOVERNOR GERINGER. I am outraged and sickened by the heinous crime committed on Matthew Shepard. I extend my most heartfelt sympathies to the family.

NEWSPERSON. Governor, you haven't pushed hate crime legislation in the past.

GOVERNOR GERINGER. I would like to urge the people of Wyoming against overreacting in a way that gives one group "special rights over others."

We will wait and see if the vicious beating and torture of Matthew Shepard was motivated by hate.

SGT. HING. You've got the beginning of the news story where they have the graphics in the background, and they've got, "Murder in Wyoming," and Wyoming's dripping red like it's got blood on it or something, and it's like what's the — what is this, this is sensationalism. And ... we're here going, "Wait a minute. We had the guys in

52

jail in less than a day, I think that's pretty damn good."

EILEEN ENGEN. And for us to be more or less maligned.

NARRATOR. Eileen and Gil Engen.

EILEEN ENGEN. That we're not a good community and we are
—- the majority of people here are good people.

GIL ENGEN. You git bad apples once in a while. And I think
that the gay community took this as an advantage, said this is a
good time for us to exploit this.

NEWSPERSON. Bill McKinney, father of one of the accused.

BILL MCKINNEY. Had this been a heterosexual, these two boys
decided to take out and rob, this never would have made the
national news. Now my son is guilty before he's even had a trial.

TIFFANY EDWARDS. Look, I do think that, um, the media
actually made people accountable. Because they made people
think. Because people were sitting in their homes, like watching
TV and listening to CNN and watching Dan Rather and going,
"Jesus Christ, well that's not how it is here." Well, how is it here?

MOMENT: MEDICAL UPDATE

NARRATOR. Matthew Shepard medical update at three P.M.,
Saturday, October tenth.

RULON STACEY. By this point, I looked out there and where
there had been two or three reporters … it must have been ten or
fifteen still photographers, another twenty or thirty reporters and
ten video cameras. The parents had just arrived. I had barely intro-
duced myself to them. I looked out there and I thought, "My
gosh. What am I going to do?" (*He crosses to the area where the
reporters are gathered with their cameras. As he arrives, several camera flashes go off. He speaks straight into the camera. We see his image
on the monitors around the stage.*)

RULON STACEY. Matthew Shepard was admitted in critical
condition approximately nine-fifteen P.M., October seventh.
When he arrived, he was unresponsive and breathing support was
being provided.

Matthew's major injuries upon arrival consisted of hypothermia and a fracture from behind his head to just in front of the right ear. This has caused bleeding in the brain, as well as pressure on the brain. There were also several lacerations on his head, face and neck.

Matthew's temperature has fluctuated over the last twenty-four hours, ranging from 98 to 106 degrees. We have had difficulty controlling his temperature.

Matthew's parents arrived at seven P.M., October ninth, and are now at his bed side. The following is a statement from them:

"First of all, we want to thank the American public for their kind thoughts about Matthew and their fond wishes for his speedy recovery. We appreciate your prayers and good will, and we know that they are something Matthew would appreciate, too.

"We also have a special request for the members of the media. Matthew is very much in need of his family at this time, and we ask that you respect our privacy, as well as Matthew's so we can concentrate all of our efforts, thoughts and love on our son.

"Thank you very much."

MOMENT: SEEING MATTHEW

NARRATOR. Both Aaron McKinney and Russell Henderson pled not guilty to charges. Their girlfriends, Chasity Pasley and Kristin Price also pled not guilty after being charged as accessories after the fact. On our next trip, we spoke with the chief investigating officer on the case, Detective Rob DeBree of the Albany County Sheriff's Department.

ROB DEBREE. I guess the thing that bothered me the most was when I went down to Poudre Valley where Matthew was and the thing that bothered me the most is seeing him, touching him. As a homicide detective, you look at bodies ... This poor boy is sitting here, fighting all his life, trying to make it. I wanted it so by the book, you know.

AARON KREIFELS. I keep seeing that picture in my head when

I found him.

NARRATOR. Aaron Kreifels.

AARON KREIFELS. And it's not pleasant whatsoever. I don't want it to be there. I wanna like get it out. That's the biggest part for me is seeing that picture in my head. And it's kind of unbelievable to me, you know, that — I happened to be the person who found him — because the big question with me, like with my religion, is like why did God want ME to find him.

CATHERINE CONNOLLY. I know how to take care of myself, and I was irrationally terrified.

NARRATOR. Catherine Connolly.

CATHERINE CONNOLLY. So what that means is, not letting my twelve-year-old son walk the streets, seeing a truck do a U-turn and thinking it's coming after me. Having to stop because I'm shaking so bad. And in fact, the pick-up truck did not come after me, but my reaction was to have my heart in my mouth.

MATT GALLOWAY. Ultimately, no matter how you dice it, I did have an opportunity.

NARRATOR. Matt Galloway.

MATT GALLOWAY. If I had — amazing hindsight of 20/20 — to have stopped — what occurred ... and I keep thinkin', "I shoulda noticed. These guys shouldn't a been talking to this guy. I shoulda not had my head down when I was washing dishes for those twenty seconds." Things I coulda done. What the hell was I thinking?

ROB DEBREE. So you do a lot of studying, you spend hours and hours and hours. You study and study and study ... talking to the officers, making sure they understand, talk to your witnesses again, and then always coming back to — I get this flash of seeing Matthew ... I wanted it so tight that there was no way that they were gonna get out of this.

REGGIE FLUTY. One of the things that happened when I got to the fence ...

NARRATOR. Reggie Fluty.

REGGIE FLUTY. It was just such an overwhelming amount of blood ... and we try to wear protective gloves, but we had a really cheap Sheriff at the time, and he bought us shit gloves, you know, you put 'em on, you put 'em on, and they kept breaking, so finally

55

you just ran out of gloves, you know. So, you figure, well, you know, "Don't hesitate," you know, that's what your mind tells you all the time. Don't hesitate, and so you just keep moving and you try to help Matthew and find an airway and you know, that's what you do, you know.

MARGE MURRAY. The thing I wasn't telling you before is that Reggie is my daughter.

NARRATOR. Marge Murray.

MARGE MURRAY. And when she first told me she wanted to be a police officer, well, I thought there was not a better choice for her. She could handle whatever came her way ...

REGGIE FLUTY. Probably a day and a half later, the hospital called me and told me Matthew had HIV. And the doctor said, "You've been exposed, and you've had a bad exposure," because you see, I'd been — been building — building a, uh, lean-to for my llamas and my hands had a bunch of open cuts on 'em, so I was kinda screwed, *(She laughs.)* you know, and you think, "Oh, shoot," you know.

MARGE MURRAY. Would you like to talk about losing sleep?

REGGIE FLUTY. So I said to the doctor okay, what do I do? And they said, "Get up here." So, I got up there and we started the ATZ [sic] drugs. Immediately.

MARGE MURRAY. Now they told me that's a medication that if it's administered thirty-six hours after you've been exposed ... it can maybe stop your getting the disease ...

REGGIE FLUTY. That is a mean, nasty medicine. Mean. I've lost ten pounds and a lot of my hair. Yeah ...

MARGE MURRAY. And quite frankly I wanted to lash out at somebody. Not at Matthew, please understand that, not one of us was mad at Matthew. But we maybe wanted to squeeze McKinney's head off. And I think about Henderson. And, you know, two absolutely human beings cause so much grief for so many people ... It has been terrible for my whole family, but mostly for her and her kids.

REGGIE FLUTY. I think it brought home to my girls what their mom does for a living.

MARGE MURRAY. Well, Reggie, you know what I'm gonna tell you now.

REGGIE FLUTY. And my parents, told me, you know, they both said the same damn thing.

MARGE MURRAY. You're quitting this damn job!

REGGIE FLUTY. And it's just a parent thing, you know, and they're terribly proud of you, 'cause you do a good job whether it's handling a drunk or handling a case like this, but you're, you know, they don't want you getting hurt —

MARGE MURRAY. Like I said, there's a right way, a wrong way, and then there's Reggie's way.

REGGIE FLUTY. So finally I said, "Oh, for God's sakes, lighten up, Francis!"

MARGE MURRAY. You are so stubborn!

REGGIE FLUTY. They say I'm stubborn and I don't believe them, but I just think, you know, okay I've heard your opinion and now here's mine, I'm thirty-nine years old, you know, what are they gonna do, spank me?

MARGE MURRAY. Reggie, don't give me any ideas.

REGGIE FLUTY. It'd look pretty funny. You know, what can they say?

MARGE MURRAY. I just hope she doesn't go before me. I just couldn't handle that.

MOMENT: E-MAIL

NARRATOR. University of Wyoming President Philip Dubois.

PHILIP DUBOIS. Well, this is a young person — who read my statement on the *Denver Post* story, and sent me an e-mail, to me directly, and said:

EMAIL WRITER. "You and the straight people of Laramie and Wyoming are guilty of the beating of Matthew Shepard just as the Germans who looked the other way are guilty of the deaths of the Jews, the Gypsies and the homosexuals. You have taught your straight children to hate their gay and lesbian brothers and sisters — unless and until you acknowledge that Matt Shepard's beating is not just a random occurrence, not just the work of a couple of random crazies, you have Matthew's blood on your hands."

PHILIP DUBOIS. And uh, well, I just can't begin to tell you what that does to you. And it's like, you can't possibly know what I'm thinking, you can't possibly know what this has done to me and my family and my community.

MOMENT: VIGILS

NARRATOR. That first week alone, vigils for Matthew Shepard were held in Laramie, Denver, Fort Collins, and Colorado Springs. Soon after, in Detroit, Chicago, San Francisco, Washington, D.C., Atlanta, Nashville, Minneapolis, and Portland, Maine, among others. In Los Angeles, 5,000 people gathered, and in New York City, a political rally ended in civil disobedience and hundreds of arrests. And the Poudre Valley Hospital web site received close to a million visitors from across the country and around the world, all expressing hope for Matthew's recovery. *(On the monitors we see images of vigils taking place around the country.)*

MOMENT: MEDICAL UPDATE

Rulon Stacey is in front of the camera. We see him on the monitor.

NARRATOR. Matthew Shepard medical update at nine A.M., Sunday, October eleventh.

RULON STACEY. As of nine A.M. today, Matthew Shepard remains in critical condition.

The family continues to emphasize that the media respect their privacy. The family also wants to thank the American public for their kind thoughts and concern for Matthew.

MOMENT: LIVE AND LET LIVE

JEDADIAH SCHULTZ. There are certain things when I sit in church.

NARRATOR. Jedadiah Schultz.

JEDADIAH SCHULTZ. And the Reverend will tell you flat out he doesn't agree with homosexuality — and I don't know — I think right now I'm going through changes. I'm still learning about myself and — you know, I don't feel like I know enough about certain things to make a decision that says, "Homosexuality is right." When you've been raised your whole life that it's wrong — and right now, I would say that I don't agree with it — yeah, that I don't agree with it, but — maybe that's just because I couldn't do it — and speaking in religious terms — I don't think that's how God intended it to happen. But I don't hate homosexuals and I mean — I'm not going to persecute them or anything like that. At all. I mean, that's not gonna be getting in the way between me and the other person at all.

CONRAD MILLER. Well, it's preached in schools that being gay is okay and yada yada, yada.

NARRATOR. Conrad Miller.

CONRAD MILLER. And if my kids asked me, I'd set them down and I'd say, "Well this is what gay people do. This is what animals do. Okay?" And I tell 'em, this is the life, this is the lifestyle, this is what they do. And I'd say, "This is why I believe it's wrong."

MURDOCK COOPER. There's more gay people around than what you think.

NARRATOR. Murdock.

MURDOCK COOPER. It doesn't bother anybody because most of 'em that are gay or lesbian, they know damn well who to talk to. If you step out of line you're asking for it. Some people are saying he made a pass at them. You don't pick up regular people. I'm not excusing their actions, but it made me feel better because it was partially Matthew Shepard's fault and partially the guys who did it ... you know maybe it's fifty-fifty.

59

ZACKIE SALMON. Yes, as a lesbian I was more concerned for my safety.

NARRATOR. Zackie Salmon.

ZACKIE SALMON. I think we all were. And I think it's because somewhere inside we all know it could happen to us anytime, you know. I mean, I would be afraid to walk down the street and display any sort of physical affection for my partner. You don't do that here in Laramie.

JONAS SLONAKER. Well, there's this whole idea: You leave me alone, I leave you alone.

NARRATOR. Jonas Slonaker.

JONAS SLONAKER. And it's even in some of the Western literature, you know, live and let live. That is such crap. I tell my friends that — even my gay friends bring it up sometimes. I'm like, "That is crap, you know?" I mean basically what it boils down to: If I don't tell you I'm a fag, you won't beat the crap out of me. I mean, what's so great about that? That's a great philosophy?

MOMENT: IT HAPPENED HERE

ZUBAIDA ULA. We went to the candle vigil.

NARRATOR. Zubaida Ula.

ZUBAIDA ULA. And it was so good to be with people who felt like shit. I kept feeling like I don't deserve to feel this bad, you know? And someone got up there and said uh — he said um, blah blah blah blah blah and then he said, I'm saying it wrong, but basically he said, c'mon guys, let's show the world that Laramie is not this kind of a town. But it is that kind of a town. If it wasn't this kind of a town, why did this happen here? I mean, you know what I mean, like — that's a lie. Because it happened here. So how could it not be a town where this kind of thing happens? Like, that's just totally — like, looking at an Escher painting and getting all confused like, it's just totally like circular logic, like how can you even say that? And we have to mourn this and we have to be sad that we live in a town, a state, a country where shit like this happens. I

60

mean, these are people trying to distance themselves from this crime. And we need to own this crime. I feel. Everyone needs to own it. We are like this. We ARE like this. WE are LIKE this.

MOMENT: SHANNON AND JEN

STEPHEN BELBER. I was at the Fireside Bar one afternoon and I ran into two friends of Aaron McKinney, Shannon and Jen. *(To Shannon and Jen.)* You knew Aaron well, right?

SHANNON. Yeah, we both did. When I first found out, I thought it was really really awful. I don't know whether Aaron was fucked up or whether he was coming down or what, but Matthew had money. Shit, he had better clothes than I did. Matthew was a little rich bitch.

JEN. You shouldn't call him a rich bitch, though, that's not right.

SHANNON. Well, I'm not saying he's a bad guy either, because he was just in the wrong place at the wrong time, said the wrong things. And I don't know. I won't lie to you, there was times that I was all messed up on meth and I thought about going out and robbing. I mean, I never did. But, yeah it was there. It's easy money.

JEN. Aaron's done that thing before. They've both done it. I know one night they went to Cheyenne to go do it and they came back with probably $300. I don't know if they ever chose like gay people as their particular targets before, but anyone that looked like they had a lot of money and that was, you know, they could outnumber, or overpower *(Pause.)* was fair game.

STEPHEN BELBER. Do you think there was any homophobia at all involved in this that contributed to some of it?

JEN. Probably. It probably would of pissed him off that Matthew was gay 'cause he didn't like — the gay people that I've seen him interact with, he was fine as long as you know, they didn't hit on him, as long as it didn't come up.

SHANNON. As long as they weren't doing it in front of him.

STEPHEN BELBER. Do you get the impression that he knew other gay people?

SHANNON. I'm sure that he knew people that are gay. I mean, he worked up at KFC and there was a couple people up there that — yeah. *(He laughs.)* And I'm not saying it's bad or anything, 'cause I don't know, half the people I know here in Laramie are gay.

STEPHEN BELBER. What would you guys say to Aaron if you saw him right now?

SHANNON. First of all, I'd ask him if he'd ever do anymore tweak.

JEN. If I saw Aaron now, I'd be like, "Man, why'd you fuck up like that?" But, I'd want to make sure he's doing good in there. But I'm sure he is, though. I'd probably just want to like hang out with him.

SHANNON. Smoke a bowl with him.

JEN. I bet he wants one so bad.

STEPHEN BELBER. You guys both went to Laramie High?

SHANNON. Yeah. Can't you tell? We're a product of our society

MOMENT: HOMECOMING

NEWSPERSON. On a day that is traditionally given over to nothing more profound than collegiate exuberance and the fortunes of the University of Wyoming football team, this community on the high plains had a different kind of homecoming Saturday, as many searched their souls in the wake of a vicious, apparent anti-gay hate crime.

NARRATOR. University President Philip Dubois.

PHILIP DUBOIS. This was Homecoming weekend. There were a lot of people in town, and there's a homecoming parade that was scheduled and then the students organized to tag onto the back of it — you know, behind the banner supporting Matt, and everybody wearing the armbands that the students had created ...

HARRY WOODS. I live in the center of town.

NARRATOR. Harry Woods.

HARRY WOODS. And my apartment has windows on two opposite streets. One goes north and one goes south. And that is exactly the Homecoming Parade route. Now, on the day of the parade, I had a cast on my leg because of a fall. So I was very disappointed because I really wanted to walk with the people that were marching for Matthew. But I couldn't. So I watched from my window. And it was … it was just … I'm fifty-two years old and I'm gay. I have lived here for many years and I've seen a lot. And I was very moved when I saw the tag on the end of the Homecoming Parade. About a hundred people walking behind a Banner for Matthew Shepard.

So then the Parade went down to the end of the block to make a U-turn and I went to the other side of my apartment to wait for it to come south down the other street.

MATT GALLOWAY. I was right up in front there where they were holding the banner for Matthew, and let me tell you … I've never had goose bumps so long in my life. It was incredible. A mass of people. Families — mothers holding their six-year-old kids, tying these arm bands around these six-year-old kids and trying to explain to them why they should wear an armband. Just amazing, I mean, it was absolutely one of the most — beautiful things I've ever done in my life.

HARRY WOODS. Well, about ten minutes went by and sure enough the parade started coming down the street. And then I noticed the most incredible thing … as the parade came down the street … the number of people walking for Matthew Shepard had grown five times. There were at least 500 people marching for Matthew. 500 people. Can you imagine? The tag at the end was larger than the entire parade. And people kept joining in. And you know what? I started to cry. Tears were streaming down my face. And I thought. Thank God that I got to see this in my lifetime. And my second thought was, "Thank you, Matthew."

MOMENT: ONE OF OURS

SHERRY JOHNSON. I really haven't been all that involved, per se. My husband's a highway patrolman, so that's really the only way that I've known about it.

Now when I first found out, I just thought it was horrible. I just, I can't ... Nobody deserves that! I don't care who ya are.

But, the other thing that was not brought out — at the same time that happened, that patrolman was killed. And there was nothing. Nothing. They didn't say anything about the old man that killed him. He was driving down the road and he shouldn't have been driving and killed him. It was just a little piece in the paper. And we lost one of our guys.

You know, my husband worked with him. This man was brand new on the force. But I mean, here's one of ours, and it was just a little piece in the paper.

And a lot of it is my feeling that the media is portraying Matthew Shepard as a saint. And making him as a martyr. And I don't think he was. I don't think he was that pure.

Now, I didn't know him, but ... there's just so many things about him that I found out that I just, it's scary. You know about his character and spreading AIDS and a few other things. You know, being the kind of person that he was, he was just a barfly, you know. And I think he pushed himself around. I think he flaunted it.

Everybody's got problems. But why they exemplified him I don't know. What's the difference if you're gay? A hate crime is a hate crime. If you murder somebody you hate 'em. It has nothing to do with if you're gay or a prostitute or whatever.

I don't understand. I don't understand.

MOMENT: TWO QUEERS
AND A CATHOLIC PRIEST

NARRATOR. Company member Leigh Fondakowski.

LEIGH FONDAKOWSKI. This is one of the last days on our second trip to Laramie. Greg and I have been conducting interviews nonstop and we are exhausted.

GREG PIEROTTI. We are to meet Father Roger at seven-thirty in the morning. I was wishing we could skip it all together, but we have to follow through to the end. So here we go. Seven-thirty A.M., two queers and a Catholic Priest.

FATHER ROGER SCHMIT. Matthew Shepard has served us well. You realize that? He has served us well. And I do not mean to condemn Matthew to perfection, but I cannot mention anyone who has done more for this community than Matthew Shepard.

And I'm not gonna sit here and say, "I was just this bold guy — no fear." I was scared — I was very vocal in this community when this happened — and I thought, "You know, should we, uh, should we call the bishop and ask him permission to do the vigil?" And I was like, "Hell, no, I'm not going to do that." His permission doesn't make it correct, you realize that? And I'm not knocking bishops, but what is correct is correct.

You people are just out here on a search though. I will do this, I will trust you people that if you write a play of this, that you *(Pause.)* say it right, say it correct. I think you have a responsibility to do that.

Don't — don't — don't, um, *(Pause.)* don't make matters worse ... You think violence is what they did to Matthew — they did do violence to Matthew — but, you know, every time that you are called a fag, or you are called a, you know, a lez or whatever ...

LEIGH FONDAKOWSKI. Or a dyke.

FATHER ROGER SCHMIT. Dyke, yeah dyke. Do you realize that is violence? That is the seed of violence. And I would resent it immensely if you use anything I said, uh, you know, to — to somehow cultivate that kind of violence, even in it's smallest form — I would resent it immensely. You need to know that.

LEIGH FONDAKOWSKI. Thank you, Father, for saying that.
FATHER ROGER SCHMIT. Just deal with what is true. You know what is true. You need to do your best to say it correct.

MOMENT: CHRISTMAS

NARRATOR. Andrew Gomez.
ANDREW GOMEZ. I was in there. I was in jail with Aaron in December. I got thrown in over Christmas. Assault and battery, two counts. I don't wanna talk about it. But we were sittin' there eatin' our Christmas dinner, tryin' to eat my stuffing, my mother-fucking bread, my little roll and what not, and I asked him, I was like, "Hey homey, tell me something, tell me something, please, why did you — " Okay, I'm thinking how I worded this, I was like "Why did you KILL a faggot if you're gonna be destined to BE a faggot later?" You know? I mean, think about it. He's either gonna get humped a lot or he's gonna die. So why would you do that? Think about that. I don't understand that.

And you know what he told me? Honest to God, this is what he said, he goes, "He tried to grab my dick." That's what he said, man! He's dumb, dog, he don't even act like it was nothin'."

Now I heard they was auctioning those boys off. Up there in the max ward, you know, where the killers go. I heard that when they found out Aaron was coming to prison, they were auctioning those boys off. "I want him. I'll put aside five, six, seven cartons of cigarettes." Auction his ass off. I'd be scared to go to prison if I was those two boys.

MOMENT: LIFESTYLE 2

BAPTIST MINISTER. Hello.

AMANDA GRONICH. Reverend?

BAPTIST MINISTER. Yes, hello.

AMANDA GRONICH. I believe your wife told you a bit about why I'm contacting you.

BAPTIST MINISTER. Yes, she did. And let me tell you — uh — I don't know that I really want to talk to anyone about any of this incident — uh — I am somewhat involved and I just don't think —

AMANDA GRONICH. Yes, I completely understand and I don't blame you. You know, I went to your service on Sunday.

BAPTIST MINISTER. You went to the services on Sunday?

AMANDA GRONICH. Yes, I did.

BAPTIST MINISTER. On Sunday?

AMANDA GRONICH. Yes, this past Sunday.

BAPTIST MINISTER. Did I meet you?

AMANDA GRONICH. Yes, you welcomed me at the beginning, I believe.

BAPTIST MINISTER. I see. Well, let me tell you. I am not afraid to be controversial or to speak my mind and that is not necessarily the views of my congregation, per se. Now as I said, I am somewhat involved — that the people in the case — well, the girlfriend of the accused is a member of our congregation, and one of the accused has visited.

AMANDA GRONICH. Mmmmmm.

BAPTIST MINISTER. Now, those two people, the accused, have forfeited their lives. We've been after the two I mentioned for ages, trying to get them to live right, to do right. Now, one boy is on suicide watch and I am working with him — until they put him in the chair and turn on the juice I will work for his salvation. Now I think they deserve the death penalty — I will try to deal with them spiritually.

AMANDA GRONICH. Right, I understand.

BAPTIST MINISTER. Now, as for the victim, I know that that

lifestyle is legal, but I will tell you one thing. I hope that Matthew Shepard as he was tied to that fence that he had time to reflect on a moment when someone had spoken the word of the Lord to him — and that before he slipped into a coma he had a chance to reflect on his lifestyle.

AMANDA GRONICH. Thank you, Reverend, I appreciate your speaking with me. *(Rain begins to fall on stage.)*

MOMENT: THAT NIGHT

RULON STACEY. About eleven-thirty that night, I had just barely gone to bed, and Margo our chief operating officer called and said, "His blood pressure has started to drop." "Well, let's wait and see." She called me about ten after — he just died. So I quick got dressed and came in. And, uh, and — and went into the ICU where the family was and Judy came up and she put her arms around me and I put my arms around her and we just stood there — honestly, for about ten minutes just — 'cause what else do you do?

And then we had to sit and talk about things that you just — "Dennis, it's now public knowledge … And I'm gonna go out there now and tell the whole world that this has happened."

'Cause by this point it was clear to us that it was the world — it was the whole world.

And so Judy told me what she wanted me to say. And I went out at four o'clock A.M. *(He crosses to the camera.)*

MOMENT: MEDICAL UPDATE

NARRATOR. Matthew Shepard medical update for four-thirty A.M., Monday, October twelfth.

RULON STACEY. *(Into the camera. We see him on the monitors.)*

68

At twelve midnight on Monday, October twelfth, Matthew Shepard's blood pressure began to drop. We immediately notified his family who were already at the hospital.

At twelve fifty-three A.M. Matthew Shepard died. His family was at his bedside.

The family did release the following statement:

The family again asked me to express their sincerest gratitude to the entire world for the overwhelming response for their son.

The family was grateful that they did not have to make a decision regarding whether or not to continue life support for their son. Like a good son, he was caring to the end and removed guilt or stress from the family.

He came into the world premature and left the world premature.

Matthew's mother said, "Go home, give your kids a hug and don't let a day go by without telling them that you love them."

MOMENT: MAGNITUDE

RULON STACEY. And — I don't know how I let that happen — I lost it on national television, but, you know, we had been up for like seventy-two hours straight and gone home and gone to sleep for half an hour and had to get up and come in — and maybe I was just way — I don't know — but *(Pause.)* in a moment of complete brain-deadness, while I was out there reading that statement I thought about my own four daughters — and go home hug your kids — *(He begins to cry.)* and oh, she doesn't have her kid anymore.

And there I am and I'm thinking "This is so lame."

Um, and then we started to get people sending us e-mails and letters. And most of them were just generally very kind. But I did get this one. This guy wrote me and said, "Do you cry like a baby on TV for all of your patients or just the faggots?" And as I told you before, homosexuality is not a lifestyle with which I agree. Um, but having been thrown into this. *(Pause.)* I guess I

69

didn't understand the magnitude with which some people hate. And of all the letters that we got, there were maybe two or three that were like that. Most of them were, thank you for your caring and compassion and Matthew had caring and compassion from the moment he got here.

MOMENT: H-O-P-E

STEPHEN BELBER. I spoke with Doc today and told him we would soon be coming back out for the upcoming trials of Russell Henderson and Aaron McKinney, and this is what he had to say: DOC O'CONNOR. I'll tell you what, if they put those two boys to death, that would defeat everything Matt would be thinking about on them. Because Matt would not want those two to die. He'd want to leave them with hope. *(Spelling.)* H-O-P-E. Just like the whole world hoped that Matt would survive. The whole thing, you see, the whole thing, ropes around hope, H-O-P-E.

End of Act Two

ACT THREE

The stage is now empty except for several chairs stage right. They are all facing the audience and arranged in rows as if to suggest a church or courthouse.

MOMENT: SNOW

MATT GALLOWAY. The day of the funeral. It was snowing so bad, big huge wet snowflakes. And when I got there, there were thousands of people in just black, with umbrellas everywhere. And there were two churches — one for the immediate family, uh, invited guests, people of that nature, and then one church for everybody else who wanted to be there. And then still, hundreds of people outside that couldn't fit into either of the churches. And there was a big park by the church, and that's where these people were. And this park was full.

PRIEST. The liturgy today is an Easter liturgy. It finds its meaning in the resurrection. The service invites your full participation.

PRIEST. The Lord be with you.

PEOPLE. And also with you

PRIEST. Let us pray

TIFFANY EDWARDS. And I guess it was like the worst storm that they have had.

NARRATOR. Tiffany Edwards.

TIFFANY. Like that anybody could ever tell, like trees fell down and the power went out for a couple of days because of it and I just thought, "It's like the forces of the universe at work, you know." Whatever higher spirit you know is like that blows storms, was blowin' this storm.

PRIEST. For our brother, Matthew, let us pray to our Lord Jesus Christ who said, "I am the Resurrection and the Life." We pray to

71

the Lord.

PEOPLE. HEAR US LORD.

PRIEST. *(The Priest begins and goes into sotto voce.)* Lord, you who consoled Martha and Mary in their distress, draw near to us who mourn for Matthew, and dry the tears of those who weep. We pray to the Lord.

PEOPLE. HEAR US LORD.

PRIEST. You wept at the grave of Lazarus, your friend. Comfort us in our sorrow. We pray to the Lord.

PEOPLE. HEAR US LORD.

PRIEST. You raised the dead to life. Give to our brother eternal life. We pray to the Lord.

PEOPLE. HEAR US LORD.

PRIEST. You promised paradise to the thief who repented; bring our brother the joys of heaven. We pray to the Lord.

PEOPLE. HEAR US LORD.

PRIEST. He was nourished with your Body and Blood; grant him a place at the table in your heavenly kingdom. We pray to the Lord.

PEOPLE. HEAR US LORD.

PRIEST. Comfort us in our sorrows at the death of our brother; let our faith be our consolation, and eternal life our hope. We pray to the Lord.

KERRY DRAKE. My most striking memory from the funeral …

NARRATOR. Kerry Drake, *Casper Star Tribune.*

KERRY DRAKE. … is seeing the Reverend Fred Phelps from Kansas … that scene go up in the park.

REV. FRED PHELPS. Do you believe the Bible? Do you believe you're supposed to separate the precious from the vile? You don't believe that part of the Bible? You stand over there ignorant of the fact that the Bible — two times for every verse it talks about God's love it talks about God's hate. *(Reverend Fred Phelps continues sotto voce.)*

KERRY DRAKE. A bunch of high-school kids who got out early came over and started yelling at some of these people in the protest — the Fred Phelps people, and across the street you had people lining up for the funeral … Well, I remember a guy, I remember this skinhead coming over and he was dressed in leather and spikes everywhere and he came over from across the street where the protest was and he came into the crowd and I just thought, oh this is gonna be a really ugly confrontation. But instead he came over and he started leading them in amazing grace. *(The people sing "Amazing Grace.")*

REV. FRED PHELPS. We wouldn't be here if this was just another murder the state was gonna deal with. The state deals with hundreds of murders every single day. But this murder is different, because the fags are bringing us out here trying to make Matthew Shepard into a poster boy for the gay lifestyle. And we're going to answer it. It's just that simple. *(Reverend Fred Phelps continues sotto voce.)*

NARRATOR. Six months later, the company returned to Laramie for the trial of Russell Henderson, the first of the two perpetrators. It was to be a capital murder trial. When we got to the Albany County Courthouse, Fred Phelps was already there.

REV. FRED PHELPS. You don't like that attribute of God.

NARRATOR. But so was Romaine Patterson.

REV. FRED PHELPS. That perfect of attribute of God. Well, *we* love that attribute of God and we're going to preach it. Because God's hatred is pure. It's a determination — it's a determination that he's gonna send some people to hell. That's God's hatred … *(Continues sotto voce.)* We're standing here with God's message. We're standing here with God's message. Is homosexuality — is being a fag okay? What do you mean it's not for you to judge? If God doesn't hate fags, why does he put 'em in hell? … You see the barrenness and sterility of your silly arguments when set over against some solid gospel truth? Barren and sterile. Like your lifestyle. Your silly arguments.

ROMAINE PATTERSON. After seeing Fred Phelps protesting at Matthew's funeral and finding out that he was coming to Laramie for the trial of Russell Henderson I decided that someone needed to stand toe to toe with this guy and show the differences. And I think at times like this when we're talking about hatred as much as the nation is right now, that someone needs to show, that there is a better way of dealing with that kind of hatred.

So our idea is to dress up like angels. And so we have designed an angel outfit — for our wings are HUGE — they're like big ass wings — and there'll be ten to twenty of us that are angels — and what we're gonna do is we're gonna encircle Phelps … and because of our big wings — we are gonna COM-PLETE-LY block him.

So this big ass band of angels comes in. We don't say a fuckin"
word. We just turn our backs to him and we stand there ... And
we are a group of people bringing forth a message of peace and
love and compassion. And we're calling it "Angel Action."

Yeah, this twenty-one-year-old little lesbian is ready to walk
the line with him.

REV. FRED PHELPS. When those old preachers laid their hands
on me it's called an ordination. Then they deliver a charge. Mine
was from Isaiah 58:1 — "Cry aloud. Spare not. Lift up thy voice
like a trumpet and show my people their transgressions."

ROMAINE PATTERSON. And I knew that my angels were
gonna be taking the brunt of everything he had to yell and say. I
mean, we were gonna be blocking his view and he was gonna be
like pissed off to all hell ... So I went out and bought all my angels
ear plugs. *("Amazing Grace" ends.)*

MOMENT: JURY SELECTION

BAILIFF. The court is in session. *(All stand.)*
NARRATOR. Romaine Patterson's sister, Trish Steger.
TRISH STEGER. As soon as they started jury selection, you
know, everybody was coming into my shop with "I don't want to
be on this trial. I hope they don't call me." Or, "Oh my God, I've
been called. How do I get off?" Just wanting to get as far away
from it as they could ... very fearful that they were going to have
to be part of that jury.

And then I heard ... Henderson had to sit in the courtroom
while they question the prospective jurors. And one of the questions
that they ask is. Would you be willing to put this person to death?

And I understand that a lot of the comments were. "Yes, I
would."
JUROR. Yes, I would, your Honor.
JUROR. Yes, sir.
JUROR. Absolutely.

JUROR. Yes, sir! *(The jurors continue underneath.)*
JUROR. No problem.
JUROR. Yep.
TRISH STEGER. Well can you imagine hearing that? You know, juror after juror after juror ...

MOMENT: RUSSELL HENDERSON

JUDGE. *("Amazing Grace" begins again.)* You entered a not guilty plea earlier, Mr. Henderson. But, I understand you wish to change your plea today; is that correct?
RUSSELL HENDERSON. Yes, sir.
JUDGE. You understand, Mr. Henderson, that the recommended sentence here is two life sentences?
RUSSELL HENDERSON. Yes, sir.
JUDGE. Do you understand that those may run concurrently or they may run consecutively?
RUSSELL HENDERSON. Yes, sir.
JUDGE. Mr. Henderson, I will now ask you how you wish to plead, guilty or not guilty?
RUSSELL HENDERSON. Guilty.
JUDGE. Before the court decides whether the sentences will be concurrent or consecutive, I understand that there are statements to be made by at least one individual.
NARRATOR. This is an excerpt from a statement made to the court by Lucy Thompson.
LUCY THOMPSON. As the grandmother and the person who raised Russell, along with my family, we have written the following statement: Our hearts ache for the pain and suffering that the Shepards have went through. We have prayed for your family since the very beginning. Many times throughout the day I have thought about Matt. And you will continue to be in our thoughts and prayers, as we know that your pain will never go away. You have showed such mercy in allowing us to have this plea, and we are so grateful that you are giving us all the opportunity to live. Your

75

Honor, we, as a family, hope that, as you sentence Russell, that you will do it concurrently two life terms. For the Russell we know and love, we humbly plead, Your Honor, to not take Russell completely out of our lives forever.

JUDGE. Thank you. Mr. Henderson, you have a constitutional right to make a statement if you would like to do so. Do you have anything you would like to say?

RUSSELL HENDERSON. Yes, I would, Your Honor. Mr. and Mrs. Shepard, there is not a moment that goes by that I don't see what happened that night. I know what I did was very wrong, and I regret greatly what I did. You have my greatest sympathy for what happened. I hope that one day you will be able to find it in your hearts to forgive me. Your Honor, I know what I did was wrong. I'm very sorry for what I did, and I'm ready to pay my debt for what I did.

JUDGE. Mr. Henderson, you drove the vehicle that took Matthew Shepard to his death. You bound him to that fence in order that he might be more savagely beaten and in order that he might not escape to tell his tale. You left him out there for eighteen hours, knowing full well that he was there. Perhaps having an opportunity to save his life, and you did nothing. Mr. Henderson, this Court does not believe that you really feel any true remorse for your part in this matter. And I wonder whether you fully realize the gravity of what you've done.

The Court finds it appropriate, therefore, that sentence be ordered as follows: As to Count Three, that being felony murder with robbery, you are to serve a period of imprisonment for the term of your natural life. On Count One, kidnapping, that you serve a period of imprisonment for the term of your natural life. Sentencing for Count One to run consecutive to sentencing for Count Three.

NARRATOR. After the hearing, we spoke with Russell Henderson's Mormon home teacher.

RUSSELL HENDERSON'S MORMON HOME TEACHER. I've known Russell's family for thirty-eight years. Russell's only twenty-one so I've known him his entire life. I ordained Russell a priest of the Mormon church, so when this happened, you can imagine — disbelief … After the sentencing … the church held a disciplinary council and the result of that meeting was to excommunicate Russell from the church. And what that means is that your name is taken off the records of the church, so you just disappear.

Russell's reaction to that was not positive. It hurt him and it hurt him too to realize at that point how serious a transgression he had committed.

But I will not desert Russell. That's a matter of my religion and my friendship with the family. *(All exit. Lights fade on Russell, his grandmother and his home teacher.)*

MOMENT: ANGELS IN AMERICA

NARRATOR. Before we left Laramie, we met again with Rebecca Hilliker at the Theater Department. She is producing *Angels in America* this year at the University.

REBECCA HILLIKER. I think that's the focus the University has taken — is that we have a lot of work to do. That we have an obligation to find ways to reach our students ... And the question is — how do we move — how do we reach a whole state where there is some really deep-seated hostility toward gays? How do you reach them?

This is the beginning ... and guess who's auditioning for the lead?

JEDADIAH SCHULTZ. MY PARENTS!

NARRATOR. Jedadiah Schultz.

JEDADIAH SCHULTZ. My parents were like, so what plays are you doing this year at school? And I was like *Angels in America* and I told them the whole list of plays. And they're like, *Angels in America*? Is that ... that play you did in high school? That scene you did in high school? And I was like, yeah. And she goes, huh, so are you gonna audition for it? And I was like, yeah. And we got in this huge argument ... and my BEST, THE BEST thing that I knew I had them on is, it was just after they had seen me in a performance of *Macbeth* and onstage like I murdered like a little kid, and Lady Macduff and these two other guys, and like and she goes, well, you know, homosexuality is a sin — she kept saying that — and I go,

77

Mom, I just played a murderer tonight. And you didn't seem to have a problem with that ...

I tell you. I've never prepared myself this much for an audition in my life. Never ever. Not even close.

ROB DEBREE. Not having to deal that much with the gay society here in Laramie.

NARRATOR. Detective Sergeant Rob DeBree.

ROB DEBREE. Well, once we started working into the case, and actually speaking to the people that were gay and finding out what their underlying fears were, well, then it sort of hit home. This is America. You don't have the right to feel that fear.

And we're still going to have people who hold with the old ideals, and I was probably one of them fourteen months ago. I'm not gonna put up with it, and I'm not going to listen to it. And if they don't like my views on it, fine. The door goes both ways. I already lost a couple of buddies. I don't care. I feel more comfortable and I can sleep at night.

REGGIE FLUTY. Well, you're tested every three months.

NARRATOR. Reggie Fluty.

REGGIE FLUTY. And I was able to have the DNA test done. And so they got me to Fort Collins. They drew the blood there, flew it to Michigan, and did all the DNA work there and — which was — a week later ... I knew I was negative for good.

MARGE MURRAY. I'll tell ya, we were all on our knees saying Hail Marys.

REGGIE FLUTY. You were just elated, you know, and you think, "Thank God!"

MARGE MURRAY. So what's the first thing she does?

REGGIE FLUTY. I stuck my tongue right in my husband's mouth. I was just happy, you know, you're just so happy. You think, "Yeah, I hope I did this service well." You know, I hope I did it with some kind of integrity. So, you're just really happy ... and my daughters just bawled.

MARGE MURRAY. They were so happy.

REGGIE FLUTY. And the force ...

MARGE MURRAY. Oh boy ...

REGGIE FLUTY. We went out and got shit faced.

MARGE MURRAY. *(Simultaneous.)* Shit faced.

REGGIE FLUTY. They all bought me drinks too, it was great ... and everybody hugged and cried and you know, I kissed everybody who walked through the door ...

MARGE MURRAY. Reggie, they don't need to know that.

REGGIE FLUTY. I didn't care if they were male or female. They each got a kiss on the lips. *(Reggie and Marge exit together, arguing as they go.)*

MARGE MURRAY. Now what part of what I just said didn't you understand?

REGGIE FLUTY. Oh, get over it, Ma!

MOMENT: A DEATH PENALTY CASE

NARRATOR. Almost a year to the day that Matthew Shepard died, the trial for Aaron James McKinney was set to begin.

CAL RERUCHA. Probably the question that most of you have in your mind is, ah, ah, how the McKinney case will proceed.

NARRATOR. Cal Rerucha, prosecuting attorney.

CAL RERUCHA. And it's the decision of the county attorney's office that that will definitely be a death penalty case.

MARGE MURRAY. Part of me wants McKinney to get it. But I'm not very proud of that. I was on and off, off and on. I can't say what I would do ... I'm too personally involved.

ZACKIE SALMON. Oh, I believe in the death penalty one hundred percent. You know, because I want to make sure that guy's ass dies. This is one instance where I truly believe with all my heart an eye for an eye, a tooth for a tooth.

MATT MICKELSON. I don't know about the death penalty. But I don't ever want to see them ever walk out of Rawlins Penitentiary. I'll pay my nickel, or whatever, my little percentage of tax, nickel a day, to make sure that his ass stays in there and never sees society again and definitely never comes into my bar again.

MATT GALLOWAY. I don't believe in the death penalty. It's too much for me. I don't believe that one person should be killed as redemption for his having killed another. Two wrongs don't make a right.

ZUBAIDA ULA. How can I protest if the Shepards want McKinney dead? I just can't interfere in that. But on a personal level, I knew Aaron in grade school. We never called him Aaron. He was called A.J. ... How can we put A.J. McKinney — how can we put A.J. McKinney to death?

FATHER ROGER SCHMIT. I think right now our most important teachers must be Russell Henderson and Aaron McKinney. They have to be our teachers. How did you learn? What did we as a society do to teach you that? See, I don't know if many people will let them be their teacher. I think it would be wonderful if the judge said, "In addition to your sentence, you must tell your story, you must tell your story."

BAILIFF. All rise. State of Wyoming vs. Aaron James McKinney docket # 6381. The Honorable Barton R. Voigt presiding. The court is in session.

MOMENT: AARON MCKINNEY

NARRATOR. During the trial of Aaron McKinney, the prosecution played a taped recording of his confession.

ROB DEBREE. My name is Rob DeBree, sergeant for the Sheriff's Office. You have the right to remain silent. Anything you say can and may be used against you in a court of law.

NARRATOR. The following is an excerpt of that confession.

ROB DEBREE. Okay, so you guys, you and Russ go to the Fireside. So you're at the Fireside by yourselves, right?

AARON MCKINNEY. Yeah.

ROB DEBREE. Okay, where do you go after you leave the Fireside?

AARON MCKINNEY. Some kid wanted a ride home.

ROB DEBREE. What's he look like?

AARON MCKINNEY. Mmm, like a queer. Such a queer dude.

ROB DEBREE. He looks like a queer?

AARON MCKINNEY. Yeah, like a fag, you know?

ROB DEBREE. Okay. How did you meet him?

AARON MCKINNEY. He wanted a ride home and I just thought, well, the dude's drunk, let's just take him home.

ROB DEBREE. When did you and Russ talk about jacking him up?

AARON MCKINNEY. We kinda talked about it at the bar.

ROB DEBREE. Okay, what happened next?

AARON MCKINNEY. We drove him out past Walmart. We got over there, and he starts grabbing my leg and grabbing my genitals. I was like, "Look, I'm not a fuckin' faggot. If you touch me again, you're gonna get it." I don't know what the hell he was trying to do, but I beat him up pretty bad. Think I killed him.

ROB DEBREE. What'd you beat him with?

AARON MCKINNEY. Blacked out. My fist. My pistol. The butt of the gun. Wondering what happened to me. I had a few beers and I don't know. It's like I could see what was going on but I don't know, it was like somebody else was doing it.

ROB DEBREE. What was the first thing that he said or that he did in the truck that made you hit him?

AARON MCKINNEY. Well, he put his hand on my leg, slid his hand like as if he was going to grab my balls.

MOMENT: GAY PANIC

ZACKIE SALMON. When that defense team argued that McKinney did what he did because Matthew made a pass at him … I just wanted to vomit because that's like saying that it's okay. It's like the Twinkie Defense, when the guy killed Harvey Milk and Moscone. It's the same thing.

REBECCA HILLIKER. As much as, uh, part of me didn't want the defense of them saying that it was a gay bashing or that it was gay panic, part of me is really grateful. Because I was really scared that in the trial they were going to try and say that it was a robbery, or it was about drugs. So when they used "gay panic" as their defense, I felt this is good, if nothing else the truth is going to be told … the truth is coming out.

ROB DEBREE. Did he ever try to defend himself against you or hit you back?

AARON MCKINNEY. Yeah, sort of. He tried his little swings or whatever but he wasn't very effective.

ROB DEBREE. Okay. How many times did you hit him inside the truck before you guys stopped where you left him?

AARON MCKINNEY. I'd say I hit him two or three times, probably three times with my fists and about six times with the pistol.

ROB DEBREE. Did he ask you to stop?

AARON MCKINNEY. Well, yeah. He was getting the shit kicked out of him.

ROB DEBREE. What did he say?

AARON MCKINNEY. After he asked me to stop most all he was doing was screaming.

ROB DEBREE. So Russ kinda dragged him over to the fence, I'm assuming, and tied him up?

AARON MCKINNEY. Something like that. I just remember Russ was laughing at first but then he got pretty scared.

ROB DEBREE. Was Matthew conscious when Russ tied him up?

AARON MCKINNEY. Yeah. I told him to turn around and don't look at my license plate number cause I was scared he would tell the police. And then I asked him what my license plate said. He read it and that's why I hit him a few more times.

ROB DEBREE. Just to be sure? *(Pause.)* So obviously you don't like gay people?

AARON MCKINNEY. No, I don't.

ROB DEBREE. Would you say you hate them?

AARON MCKINNEY. Uh, I really don't hate them but, you know, when they start coming onto me and stuff like that I get pretty aggravated.

ROB DEBREE. Did he threaten you?

AARON MCKINNEY. This gay dude?

ROB DEBREE. Yeah.

AARON MCKINNEY. Not really.

ROB DEBREE. Can you answer me one thing? Why'd you guys take his shoes?

AARON MCKINNEY. I don't know. Now I'll never get to see my son again.

ROB DEBREE. I don't know. You'll probably go to court some-time today.

AARON MCKINNEY. Today? So I'm gonna go in there and just plead guilty or not guilty today?

ROB DEBREE. No, no, you're just going to be arraigned today.

AARON MCKINNEY. He is gonna die for sure?

ROB DEBREE. There is no doubt that Mr. Shepard is going to die.

AARON MCKINNEY. So what are they going to give me, twenty five to life or just the death penalty and get it over with?

ROB DEBREE. That's not our job. That's the judge's job and the jury.

MOMENT: THE VERDICT

BAILIFF. Has the jury reached a verdict?

FOREPERSON. We have, your Honor

We the jury, impaneled and sworn to try the above-entitled case, after having well and truly tried the matter, unanimously find as follows:

As to the charge of kidnapping, we find the defendant, Aaron James McKinney, guilty.

As to the charge of aggravated robbery, we find the defendant, Aaron James McKinney, guilty.

As to the charge of first-degree felony murder (kidnapping), we find the defendant, Aaron James McKinney, guilty. *(Verdict goes sotto voce. Narration begins.)*

As to the charge of first-degree felony murder (robbery), we find the defendant, Aaron James McKinney, guilty.

As to the charge of premeditated first-degree murder, we find the defendant, Aaron James McKinney, not guilty.

As to the lesser-included offense of second-degree murder, we find the defendant, Aaron James McKinney, guilty.

MOMENT: DENNIS SHEPARD'S STATEMENT

NARRATOR: Aaron McKinney was found guilty of felony murder which meant the jury could give him the death penalty. That evening, Judy and Dennis Shepard were approached by McKinney's defense team, who pled for their client's life. The prosecution indicated that they would defer to the family's wishes as to whether or not to pursue the death penalty. The following morning, Dennis Shepard made a statement to the court. Here is some of what he said:

DENNIS SHEPARD. My son Matthew did not look like a winner. He was rather uncoordinated and wore braces from the age of thirteen until the day he died. However, in his all too brief life he proved that he was a winner. On October sixth, 1998 my son tried to show the world that he could win again. On October twelfth, 1998 my first born son and my hero, lost. On October twelfth, 1998 my first born son and my hero, died, fifty days before his twenty-second birthday.

I keep wondering the same thing that I did when I first saw him in the hospital. What would he have become? How could he have changed his piece of the world to make it better?

Matt officially died in a hospital in Ft. Collins, Colorado. He actually died on the outskirts of Laramie, tied to a fence. You Mr. McKinney with your friend Mr. Henderson left him out there by himself, but he wasn't alone. There were his lifelong friends with him, friends that he had grown up with. You're probably wondering who these friends were. First he had the beautiful night sky and the same stars and moon that we used to see through a telescope. Then he had the daylight and the sun to shine on him. And through it all he was breathing in the scent of pine trees from the snowy range. He heard the wind, the ever-present Wyoming wind, for the last time. He had one more friend with him. He had God. And I feel better knowing he wasn't alone.

Matt's beating, hospitalization and funeral focused worldwide attention on hate. Good is coming out of evil. People have said enough is enough. I miss my son, but I am proud to be able to say that he is my son.

Judy has been quoted as being against the death penalty. It has been stated that Matt was against the death penalty. Both of these statements are wrong. Matt believed that there were crimes and incidents that justified the death penalty. I too believe in the death penalty. I would like nothing better than to see you die, Mr. McKinney. However this is the time to begin the healing process. To show mercy to someone who refused to show any mercy. Mr. McKinney, I am going to grant you life, as hard as it is for me to do so, because of Matthew. Every time you celebrate Christmas, a birthday, the Fourth of July remember that Matt isn't. Every time you wake up in your prison cell remember that you had the opportunity and the ability to stop your actions that night. You robbed me of something very precious and I will never forgive you for that. Mr. McKinney, I give you life in the memory of one who no longer lives. May you have a long life and may you thank Matthew every day for it.

MOMENT: AFTERMATH

REGGIE FLUTY. Me and Debree hugged and cried ... And you know everybody had tears in their eyes, and you're just so thankful you know and Mr. Shepard was cryin' and then that got me bawlin' and everybody just —·

ROB DEBREE. This is all we've lived and breathed for a year. Daily. This has been my case daily. And now it's over.

REGGIE FLUTY. Maybe now we can go on and we can quit being stuck, you know?

AARON KREIFELS. It just hit me today, the minute that I got out of the courthouse. That the reason that God wanted me to

85

find him is, for he didn't have to die out there alone, you know. And if I wouldn't've came along, they wouldn't've found him for a couple of weeks at least. So it makes me feel really good that he didn't have to die out there alone.

MATT GALLOWAY. I'm just glad it's over. I really am. Testifying in that trial was one of the hardest things I've ever done. And don't get me wrong, I love the stage, I really do I love it. But it's tricky because basically what you have is lawyers questioning you from this angle but the answers need to be funneling this way, to the jury. So what you have to do is establish a funneling system. And that's hard for me because I'm a natural conversationalist, so it's just natural instinct that when someone asks you a question, you look at that person to make eye contact. But it's kind of tough when you literally have to scoot over — change your position, in effect, funnel over to where the jury is. But I was able to do that several times over the course of my testimony. *(They are amused and baffled by this last text.)*

MOMENT: EPILOGUE

ANDY PARIS. On our last trip, I had the good fortune of seeing Jedadiah Schultz play the role of Prior in *Angels in America*. After a performance, we spoke.

JEDADIAH SCHULTZ. I didn't for the longest time let myself become personally involved in the Matthew Shepard thing. It didn't seem real. It just seemed way blown out of proportion. Matthew Shepard was just a name instead of an individual ...

I don't know. It's weird. It's so weird, man. I just — I just feel bad. Just for all that stuff I told you, for the person I used to be. That's why I want to hear those interviews from last year when I said all that stuff. I don't know. I just can't believe I ever said that stuff about homosexuals, you know. How did I ever let that stuff make me think that you were different from me?

NARRATOR. This is Romaine Patterson.

ROMAINE PATTERSON. Well, a year ago, I wanted to be a rock star. That was my goal. And now um, well, now it's obviously changed in the fact that um, throughout the last year I — I've really realized my role in, um, in taking my part. And, um, so now instead of going to school to be in music, I'm gonna go to school for communications and political science. Um, because I have a career in political activism.

Actually, I just recently found out I was gonna be honored in Washington, D.C. from the Anti-Defamation League. And whenever I think about the angels or any of the speaking that I've done, you know ... Matthew gave me — Matthew's like guiding this little path with his light for me to walk down. And he just — every time we get to like a door, he opens it. And he just says, "Okay, next step."

And if I get to be a rock star on the side, okay.

NARRATOR. This is Jonas Slonaker.

JONAS SLONAKER. Change is not an easy thing, and I don't think people were up to it here. They got what they wanted. Those two boys got what they deserve, and we look good now. Justice has been served. The OK corral. We shot down the villains. We sent the prostitutes on the train. The towns cleaned up and we don't need to talk about it anymore.

You know, it's been a year since Matthew Shepard died, and they haven't passed shit in Wyoming ... at a state level, any town, nobody anywhere, has passed any kind of laws, anti-discrimination laws or hate crime legislation, nobody has passed anything anywhere. What's come out of it? What's come out of this that's concrete or lasting?

NARRATOR. We all said we would meet again — one last time at the fence.

DOC O'CONNOR. I been up to that site in my limousine, okay? And I remembered to myself the night he and I drove around together, he said to me, "Laramie sparkles, doesn't it?" And where he was up there, if you sit exactly where he was, up there, Laramie sparkles from there, with a low lying cloud ... It's the blue lights that's bouncing off the clouds from the airport and it goes tst tst tst tst ... right over the whole city. I mean it blows you away ... Matt was right there in that spot, and I can just picture in his eyes, I can just picture what he was seeing. The last thing he saw on this earth was the sparkling lights.

MOMENT: DEPARTURE

MOISÉS KAUFMAN. We've spent the last two days packing a year's worth of materials and saying our goodbyes. We've been here six times and conducted over two hundred interviews. Jedadiah cried when he said goodbye.

LEIGH FONDAKOWSKI. Marge wished us luck and when we asked her how Laramie would feel seeing a play about itself, she said:

MARGE MURRAY. I think we'd enjoy it. To show it's not the hellhole of the earth would be nice, but that is up to how you portray us. And that in turn is up to how Laramie behaves.

GREG PIEROTTI. As we were getting off the phone she said to me:

MARGE MURRAY. Now, you take care. I love you, honey.

STEPHEN BELBER. Doc asked me if I wanted to ghost write a book about the whole event. Galloway offered me or anyone else, a place to stay if and when we come back to Laramie. He also seemed interested as to whether there'd be any open auditions for this play.

ANDY PARIS. We left Laramie at about seven in the evening. On the way to Denver, I looked in my rear view mirror to take one last look at the town.

FATHER ROGER SCHMIT. And I will speak with you, I will trust that if you write a play of this, that you say it right. You need to do your best to say it correct.

ANDY PARIS. And in the distance I could see the sparkling lights of Laramie, Wyoming.

End of Play